I0884443

Weapons of the Battle of the Bulge

Weapons of the Battle of the Bulge

From the Photographic Archives of the US Army Signal Corps

Darren Neely

Pen & Sword
MILITARY

First published in Great Britain in 2023 by
Pen & Sword Military
An imprint of
Pen & Sword Books Ltd
Yorkshire – Philadelphia

Copyright © Darren Neely 2023

ISBN 978 1 39900 105 2

The right of Darren Neely to be identified as Author of this work has been asserted by him in accordance with the Copyright, Designs and Patents Act 1988.

A CIP catalogue record for this book is available from the British Library.

All rights reserved. No part of this book may be reproduced or transmitted in any form or by any means, electronic or mechanical including photocopying, recording or by any information storage and retrieval system, without permission from the Publisher in writing.

Typeset by Mac Style
Printed in the UK by CPI Group (UK) Ltd, Croydon, CR0 4YY.

FSC www.fsc.org MIX Paper | Supporting responsible forestry FSC® C013604

Pen & Sword Books Limited incorporates the imprints of Atlas, Archaeology, Aviation, Discovery, Family History, Fiction, History, Maritime, Military, Military Classics, Politics, Select, Transport, True Crime, Air World, Frontline Publishing, Leo Cooper, Remember When, Seaforth Publishing, The Praetorian Press, Wharncliffe Local History, Wharncliffe Transport, Wharncliffe True Crime, White Owl and After the Battle.

For a complete list of Pen & Sword titles please contact

PEN & SWORD BOOKS LIMITED
47 Church Street, Barnsley, South Yorkshire, S70 2AS, England
E-mail: enquiries@pen-and-sword.co.uk
Website: www.pen-and-sword.co.uk

Or

PEN AND SWORD BOOKS
1950 Lawrence Rd, Havertown, PA 19083, USA
E-mail: Uspen-and-sword@casematepublishers.com
Website: www.penandswordbooks.com

Contents

Acknowledgements

The majority of these photographs are from the official US Army cameramen from the 165th, 166th and 167th Signal Photographic Companies attached to various army units during the Battle of the Bulge. Unless otherwise noted, all photographs are official US Army Signal Corps photos. The National Archives is the primary holder of these photographs with some housed at other institutions around the country.

For assistance in finding official signal corps photographs, I would like to thank the staff at the Still Pictures Branch at the National Archives, Fort Benning and Stanford University. A good portion of the material assembled could not have been possible without the assistance of Steve Zaloga and Lee Archer for use of photos from their personal collection and also their masterful knowledge of events and units of the Battle of the Bulge. Lastly, I would be remiss not to thank my wife Debbie and children, Annie and Aidan for their patience as I assembled these photos and wrote the description of each photo.

Introduction

Weapons of the Battle of the Bulge: Through the Eyes of the US Army Signal Corps Cameramen

The Battle of the Bulge continues to inspire and draw the interest of the military history community. Yet, and partly due to the success of Band of Brothers, when people hear the words "Battle of the Bulge", they immediately think of paratroopers holding Bastogne and then Patton's tanks riding to the rescue. The fighting in the Ardennes was so much more than that and involved hundreds of thousands of soldiers on each side. In addition, it is forgotten that British and Canadians fought in the Bulge as well on the Northern shoulder. The Bulge battles are well known for the tanks of both sides trudging through the snow but like many engagements of World War II, it was also fought and won by the soldier with the rifle, a machine-gun team, a well-coordinated mortar assault and infantry support weapons. This book is not a summary of the Bulge battles nor a tactical history as there have been numerous excellent accounts already published that capture that theme. This book will showcase all the weapons used by the soldiers in the Bulge. From rifles and heavy machine guns and mortars and artillery, and to include armored cars, self-propelled artillery and tanks this book will show how the battle was won from the M1 rifle of the frozen GI, to the expertly directed artillery strikes and to the whitewashed armored vehicles that were attacking through the snowstorms of the Belgium and Luxembourg countryside. Outside of those German weapons and vehicles captured by the Americans during the battles, the number of pictures presented here tend to favor the Americans. This is also due to the basic fact that the Americans had many more cameramen following the units into battle during these battles as compared to the Germans.

This book is broken down into three chapters. The first chapter will deal with infantry weapons and those in the infantry support role. The second chapter will feature artillery pieces and the third chapter will cover armored fighting vehicles, from armored cars to the massive German Tiger 2 tanks. I used basic reference when referring to American and German tanks and didn't bother with the exact model of tank as this book is meant to show photos of the weapons involved, not a detailed technical study of armor. When possible, the caption of the official photograph was used with additional relevant information provided by the author to put the photo in context and/or provide interesting background information.

The Battle of the Bulge, also known as the Ardennes Offensive, was the last major German offensive campaign on the Western Front during World War II. The offensive was carried out from 16 December 1944 to 25 January 1945. It was launched through the densely forested Ardennes region between Belgium and Luxembourg. Although the Germans managed to begin their offensive with complete surprise and enjoyed some initial successes, they were not able to seize the initiative on the Western Front. While the German command did not reach its goals, the Ardennes operation inflicted heavy losses and set back the Allied invasion of Germany by several weeks. However, unlike the Allies, the Germans could not replace the manpower and equipment they lost in the Bulge battles. This failed offensive in addition to the failed offensive in the south under Operation Nordwind by the Germans, were the last times the Germans could field an offensive of any kind on the Western Front. Casualty estimates for the battle vary widely. According to the US Department of Defense, American forces suffered 89,500 casualties including 19,000 killed, 47,500 wounded and 23,000 missing. The Battle of the Bulge was the bloodiest battle for US forces in World War II. British casualties totaled 1,400 with 200 deaths. The German High Command estimated that they lost between 81,834 and 98,024 men in the Bulge between 16 December 1944 and 28 January 1945. The American tank and tank destroyer losses have been put at over 700 while the Germans lost over 550 tanks and self-propelled guns.

Chapter 1

Infantry Weapons

The Battle of the Bulge was fought with the rifle of the infantryman all the way to the massive Tiger II tanks of the Germans. Yet, when the tanks rolled into a town, it was the infantrymen riding on the back armed with rifles and machine guns that jumped off and cleared the houses, trenches and other enemy positions. The artillery would provide smoke, covering fire and counter battery fire, but it was the infantrymen with their weapons and supporting heavy machine guns that were clearing the enemy out.

The weapon most photographed with the American soldier in the Ardennes was the M1 Garand rifle. Other soldiers were armed with carbines and most squads had a Browning Automatic Rifle as support. Machine guns, both .30 and .50 caliber provided additional infantry support and were also mounted on jeeps. In the following photos, you will see how the machine guns were typically positioned at roadblocks, important tactical positions and used in the supporting role for attacking infantrymen. The freezing conditions the soldiers were faced with in the Bulge battles required continuous care and cleaning of their weapons to ensure they remained in working order. The following photos in this chapter cover rifles, carbines, sub-machine guns, light and heavy machine guns and even .50 caliber water cooled machine guns used in the anti-aircraft role.

A soldier from the 106th Infantry Division showcases a new snow cape in Belgium on December 15, 1944. He is armed with a M1 rifle and has added some white material to the barrel for extra camouflage.

This GI from the 324th Combat Engineer Battalion of the 99th Infantry armed with a M1 rifle takes a knee as he communicates on the radio.

Another radioman, this soldier from the 26th Infantry Regiment of the 1st Infantry Division waits for the next message as his column advances near a blown aqueduct bridge.

A common scene in the beginning of the Battle of the Bulge, MP armed with a M1 rifle checking the identification of a soldier driving a jeep.

These three soldiers of the 28th Infantry Division were actually photographed with the soldiers of Task Force Hogan when they returned to friendly lines after being trapped behind enemy lines for a few days in the beginning days of the battles. Two of the men are armed with M1 rifles while the man on the left has a M3 submachine gun or "grease gun".

GI from the 1st Infantry Division cleans his M1 rifle during some spare moments in Nidrum, Belgium in late December 1944.

Infantry of the 4th Armored march across snowy fields on the way towards Bastogne. The man in the front carries an M1 rifle.

A photo from the same series as the one above and maybe one that might be staged a bit. GIs stand and take aim at the enemy with their M1 rifles.

Three soldiers heavily laden with ammo and packs take a rest in a small town past Malmedy in late December 1944. All three are armed with M1 rifles, bandoliers and grenades.

A soldier from the 4th Armored Division with a M1 slung across his shoulder casually watches a burning vehicle near Bastogne on 12/30/44.

A patrol of 4th Armored Division soldiers armed with M1 rifles cautiously make their way through a Belgian forest on the outskirts of Bastogne.

Two soldiers of the 36th Armored Infantry Regiment, 3rd Armored Division man snowy position with a M1 rifle and bazooka as they point towards the German lines near the end of the Battle of the Bulge, 1/17/45.

11th Infantry Regiment, 5th Infantry Division soldiers wearing white camouflage capes advance or rather pose for the cameraman outside of Haller, Luxembourg on January 1, 1945.

A solider from the 291st Infantry Regiment, 75th Infantry Division armed with a M1 rifle with a rifle grenade attached, checks the papers of a jeep driver. Interestingly enough the jeep belongs to the camera team that took this photo based on the name of Milo Laurence on the bag in the back of the jeep.

A tough looking bunch of 508th Parachute Infantry Regiment soldiers of the 82nd Airborne prepare to move out in Belgium. They are armed with a mix of M1 carbines and M1 rifles.

Outside of Devantave, Belgium soldiers with the 75th Infantry Division take aim and provide covering fire with M1s for their fellow soldiers.

A member of the 83rd Infantry Division digs ice out of his canteen after returning from the front lines near Lierneux Belgium.

Sergeant Clarence Mageriea of the 83rd Infantry Division guards his two German prisoners with his M1 rifle in Sart, Belgium on January 9, 1945.

Two soldiers with the 83rd Infantry Division take a rest and pose for the cameraman near Ottre Belgium in January 1945. The soldier on the left is armed with a M1 rifle and two grenades. The soldier on the right has a captured German reversible hood for extra warmth and comfort.

These two soldiers from an infantry unit take a warm break in a cozy stable with a cow to read letters from home. They are both armed with M1 rifles.

Pfc Frank Vukasin of the 331st Infantry Regiment, 83rd Infantry Division, loads a new clip in his M1 rifle in front of two dead German soldiers outside of Houffalize, Belgium on January 15, 1945.

Armed with a M1 rifle and .45 caliber pistol in a shoulder holster, Private Jose Viramon of the 507th Parachute Regiment of the 17th Airborne, slogs through the rubble of La Roche Belgium on his way to meet with a patrol of the First Army, thus linking them with the Third Army.

Squad of GIs with M1 rifles march through the woods near the end of the Battle of the Bulge in Luxembourg.

American soldiers armed with M1 rifles watch a captured German soldier remove the American issued pants and boots he was wearing. Being caught in American gear would put this German soldier in a precarious position.

GIs on a rooftop in Belgium reload and prepare to return fire against the enemy from a rooftop.

A M1 rifle serves as the marking point of a fallen American soldier in the deep snow somewhere in the Ardennes area during the Battle of the Bulge.

American soldier draped in a white camouflage cape and armed with a M1 rifle shows how well the white cape hides him against the deep snow in the Ardennes.

A group of exhausted soldiers of the 28th Infantry Division listen to a soldier armed with a M1 carbine after the retreat from Wiltz to the Bastogne area on December 20, 1944.

Two more soldiers from the 28th Infantry Division rest in Bastogne after retreating there during the early days of the Ardennes offensive. The soldier on the left has a M1 carbine slung on his shoulder with an ammunition pouch attached to the butt for easy access.

Soldiers from "Hogan's 400" rest in a farmyard in Soy, Belgium after their escape to friendly lines around Christmas Day 1944. Their faces are blackened for camouflage through enemy lines and the soldier on the right has a M1 carbine.

Two MPs with the 84th Division and armed with M1 carbines stop a Belgian priest and inspect his papers near Marche, Belgium in December 1944.

A soldier in regular issued gear and armed with a M1 carbine, kneels behind a soldier draped in a white cape to show how effective the white capes were as camouflage in the snowy terrain.

A soldier with the 87th Infantry Division and armed with a M1 carbine scans the front through a destroyed building in Moircy, Luxembourg on December 31, 1944.

A soldier with the 643rd Tank Destroy Battalion and armed with a M1 carbine inspects an abandoned German dugout near Reharmont, Belgium on January 6, 1945.

Two GIs of the 23rd Infantry Regiment, 2nd Infantry Division share a light moment during a lull in the fighting near Berg, Belgium. The soldier on the bicycle has a M1 carbine over his back and another carbine lays upright outside of the soldiers dugout.

A soldier prepares to load a new a magazine into his Browning Automatic Rifle (BAR) in a snowy setting somewhere in the Ardennes Forest.

Outside of Beffe, Belgium, a group of American soldiers from the 75th Infantry Division fire back at German snipers, according to the official caption. The man standing is firing back with a BAR.

Near Doncols, Luxembourg, Private William Birthold of the 357th Infantry Regiment, 90th Infantry Division takes a rest with a heavy pack and his BAR.

A soldier with the 1st Infantry Division takes a break to write letters home with his trusty BAR propped up next to him. Notice the axe behind the rifle as well. Location is Nidrum, Belgium on December 27, 1944.

Two GIs of the 101st Infantry Regiment, 26th Infantry Division share a smoke somewhere in Wiltz, Luxembourg in late January 1945. The man on the left is armed with a M3 submachine gun, or "grease gun".

A soldier with the 325th Glider Infantry Regiment peers around the back wheel of a German tractor with his M3 submachine gun somewhere in Belgium during the Battle of the Bulge.

A soldier with the 82nd Airborne Division and armed with a Thompson submachine gun guards a captured German soldier in La Fosse, Belgium on January 1, 1945.

Private Thomas Amick of the 329th Infantry Regiment, 83rd Infantry Division poses with his Thompson submachine gun with two magazines taped together in Rochefort, Belgium on January 6, 1945.

American soldier with a Thompson submachine gun peers inside a knocked out American half-track. Note the .50 caliber machine gun belts draped over the rear door of the vehicle.

GI with a Thompson submachine gun also with the double taped magazine featured carefully inspects a German soldier who appears to be frozen. The soldier might be inspecting carefully in case the German corpse was boobytrapped.

Another photo showing men of the 17th Airborne and 24th Cavalry Squadron meeting up to solidify the First and Third Army near La Roche, Belgium. Four of the five men are armed with Thompson submachine guns.

Two of the men from the previous photograph pose for a closeup which shows the soldier on the left with coveralls and the paratrooper on the right with binoculars and a Thompson submachine gun.

Sergeant Fred Hallow of the 507th Parachute Infantry Regiment, 17th Airborne Division and part of the meet up patrol, poses with his Thompson SMG. Note his knife placed near his boot.

Not be forgotten for their role in the Bulge battles, but the Canadian and British units served a part as well. Here Canadian paratroopers armed with rifles and a bren light machine gun pause for a smoke as they advance near Marche, Belgium on January 9, 1945.

British soldiers of the 51st Highland Division set demolition charges on a tree to be used on a road block near Liege, Belgium in January 1945.

Another photo of Canadian paratroopers moving near Marche, armed with a mix of Lee Enfield rifles and Sten submachine guns.

A soldier from the 771st Tank Battalion looks over an abandoned American halftrack of the 3rd Armored Division in Marcouray, Belgium. The vehicle would have belonged to the men of Task Force Hogan and was destroyed when they had to return to friendly lines on foot.

A famous photo from the Battle of the Bulge shows a German grenadier near Poteau, after an ambush on American forces. He is armed with a Sturmgewehr 44 assault rifle.

A dead German soldier lays near his MG 42 machine gun on the side of a snowy road somewhere in Belgium. Note that his helmet had been covered with white for camouflage.

American soldiers fire German weapons captured during the Bulge battles. In the foreground a soldier rips off rounds from a MG 42 while in the center a GI reloads another round in the German rifle he has confiscated.

Somewhere in Belgium an American soldier with a .30 caliber M1919 Browning machine gun, maintains a roadblock position while his comrades check the papers of a soldier in a jeep.

Two soldiers of the 2nd Infantry Division man a position with a carbine, bazooka and .30 caliber machine gun somewhere on the Belgian front on January 5, 1945.

A paratrooper with Company F, 2nd Battalion, 502nd Parachute Regiment, 101st Airborne Division mans his foxhole with a .30 caliber M1919 Browning machine gun near Bastogne on January 5, 1945.

Another view of the same foxhole as above and a bazooka, rifle, rifle clips, a box for .30 caliber machine gun rounds and ration boxes can now be seen in the photograph.

Two glider infantry soldiers of the 325th Glider Infantry Regiment stand guard with their .30 caliber machine gun near Odrimont, Belgium on January 6, 1945. The 325th was part of the 82nd Airborne Division.

A little Belgian boy watches with curiosity as an American soldier cleans the barrel of a .30 caliber machine gun near a crossroads checkpoint in Samree, Belgium in January 1945.

Two men of the 25th Armored Engineer Battalion of the 6th Armored Division show off the .30 caliber machine gun they used to hold 40 Germans when they were surrounded in a small village 3 miles east of Bastogne in January 1945.

Near Goesdorf, Luxembourg in January 1945, men of the 26th Infantry Division take a break to read the comics. Behind them is a .30 caliber machine gun post protected by rocks and a nice ad-hoc roof to protect them from the elements.

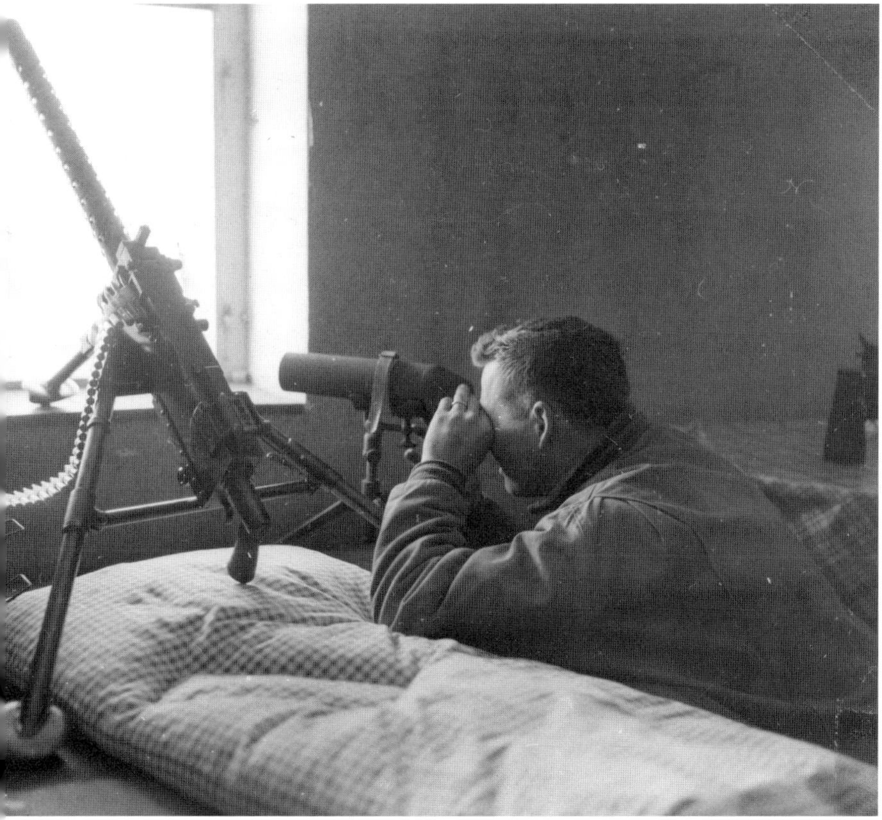

A soldier scans the front while his trusty .30 caliber machine gun stands by for enemy movement during the Bulge battles.

Manning a foxhole with a .30 caliber machine gun are two soldiers of the 48th Armored Infantry Battalion of the 7th Armored Division near St. Vith, Belgium on January 24, 1945 near the very end of hostilities in the Bulge.

One can imagine carrying the weight of this .30 caliber water cooled machine gun. This soldier is taking a well deserved rest as he moves up as part of a machine gun crew somewhere in Belgium.

With tanks in the background, this 4th Armored Division machine gun crew scans the front for enemy movement near Bastogne. Their .30 caliber water cooled machine gun shows signs of the icy and snowy elements they were currently facing.

A soldier from the 23rd Armored Engineer Battalion of the 3rd Armored Division stands guard with a .30 caliber machine gun in front of a well camouflaged tank in Ny, Belgium.

Private Charles Preston of the 11th Infantry Regiment of the 5th Infantry Division removes snow off his .30 caliber water cooled machine gun that is mounted on his jeep. This photo was taken on December 21, 1944 as his unit was moving towards Luxembourg to meet the German assault.

A GI mans his .50 caliber water cooled machine gun being used in the anti-aircraft role. Note the spare drums of rounds just outside his log covered position.

Machine gunners of Company M, 334th Infantry, 84th Infantry Division move up in Belgium on January 14, 1945. In the photo we can see a man carrying spare boxes of machine gun rounds, one man carrying the tripod and the man in the rear has the actual gun slung over his shoulder.

Great view showing the details of the .30 caliber water cooled machine gun, this one equipped with a flash suppressor. These soldiers manning a window position are with the 75th Infantry Division in Salmchateau, Belgium on January 16, 1945.

A lone machine gunner mans his .30 caliber water cooled machine gun somewhere on the 30th Infantry Division front in Belgium in January 1945.

Machine gunners from the 1st Battalion, 329th Infantry Regiment, 83rd Infantry Division stand guard with their .30 caliber water cooled machine gun in Bovigny, Belgium on January 20, 1945.

This photo might be the same crew as the previous one but from a different angle. The photo number written by the photographer is just one after the previous. A nice view of the machine gun belt that was fed into the .30 caliber machine gun.

On a hillside, a machine gun crew of the 290th Regiment, 75th Infantry Division covers the advance of infantrymen near Devantave, Belgium on January 6, 1945.

Soldier with an anti-aircraft unit attached to the 1st Infantry Division stands by his .50 caliber water cooled machine gun named "Cognac" in Berg, Belgium, January 1945.

Another .50 caliber water cooled machine gun being used in anti-aircraft role during the Battle of the Bulge.

Men of the 811th Tank Destroyer Battalion man a roadblock armed with a .50 caliber machine gun in the vicinity of Harinsart, Belgium on January 1, 1945.

In Sourbrodt, Belgium a soldier with the 1st Infantry Division removes the canvas cover from his .50 caliber machine gun installed on a ring mount of his truck.

A soldier from an assault gun platoon of the 4th Armored Division stands guard against German aircraft with his .50 caliber machine gun mounted on a M4 105mm Assault Gun.

Three members of the 30th Signal Company in their truck named "St. Lo" reload their .50 caliber machine gun after firing at six German ME-109 planes that had strafed them somewhere in Belgium on December 31, 1944.

In a foxhole with a .50 caliber machine gun, two soldiers of the 90th Infantry Division watch the front and read the news somewhere near the front lines during the Bulge battles.

A crew of a .50 caliber machine gun being used in the anti-aircraft role dig in the frozen ground near Freyneux, Belgium on January 9, 1945. The men are with the 195th Field Artillery Battalion.

Another photo of the same crew digging in for their .50 caliber machine gun position with one of their artillery pieces visible in the background.

Two soldiers from the 26th Infantry Division stand guard and pose for the cameraman with their .50c caliber machine gun in Goesdorf, Luxembourg on January 5, 1945.

A member of the 6th Armored Division works on the frozen .50 caliber machine gun atop a tank near Trois Vierges, Luxembourg. The soldier is with Company B of the 68th Tank Battalion. White washed M4 tanks can be seen in the background.

Barely visible in the snowy landscape is a soldier in a foxhole manning a .50 caliber machine gun somewhere in Belgium during the Battle of the Bulge. This photo shows perfectly the horrid weather conditions the soldiers faced during the battle.

Chapter 2

Infantry Support Weapons and Artillery

Key to the success of the infantry unit in battle was their support weapons from other men in their unit or attached units. From engineers laying anti-tank and anti-personnel mines, to bazookas to counter armored vehicles, support weapons were critical. Another common scene in the Ardennes, especially in the beginning as the Allies attempted to stem the rapid advance of the Germans was to use explosives to demolish trees to block various roadway advances to the enemy. In addition, mortars could provide smoke to conceal advances or even retreats. The mortars also provided excellent offensive fire when attempting to take the next town or flush the enemy from a wooded position. The Americans also used the quad .50 caliber mount in both the anti-aircraft and anti-personnel role to great effect.

The artillery used in the Ardennes ranged from 40mm anti-aircraft Bofors weapons to 90mm anti-aircraft guns put in the anti-tank role. From small 57mm anti-tank guns used by the Americans to the dreaded German 88mm, crews of the armored vehicles from both sides were on constant watch for that hidden anti-tank gun. American artillery ranged from the compact 75mm pack howitzer all the way to the massive 8 inch and 240mm artillery pieces. The Americans captured many German artillery pieces that were either destroyed or simply lacked the transport to move them during the retreat once the American counteroffensive started. You will also see the creative ways and great lengths the soldiers went to camouflage their weapons in the snowy landscape. The photos in this chapter show all these weapons, many in action.

In the early days of the Ardennes Offensive, replacements are trained on the use of a bazooka in the First Army sector.

A soldier with the 36th Armored Infantry Regiment of the 3rd Armored Division guards a road junction near Manhay, Belgium with his bazooka in December of 1944.

A bazooka crew prepares their weapon for action while warming themselves near a fire in Belgium. A bazooka rocket lays near their feet.

Outside of Grandmenil, Belgium, an American bazooka crew uses an abandoned German Panther tank as target practice during a lull in the fighting.

Infantry replacements from the 53rd Armored Infantry Battalion of the 4th Armored Division use a knocked out German Mark IV tank as target practice on January 5, 1945.

A close up of the same crew of the 53rd Armored Infantry as seen in the previous photograph. The soldier firing the weapon takes careful aim while his comrade serves as a spotter.

Staff Sergeant Robert Trevellin of Richmond, VA fired four different weapons during an enemy counterattack in Rochefort, Belgium in January 1945. He served with the 329th Infantry Regiment of the 83rd Infantry Division and used a carbine, M1 rifle, BAR and then the bazooka that he is holding on a Panzer IV tank.

Pfc Vernon Haught of Arizona of the 325th Glider Infantry of the 82nd Airborne returns to the rear with his bazooka after his turn at guard at an outpost near Odrimont, Belgium on January 6, 1945.

Two soldiers of the First Army in Schoppen, Belgium examine a German bazooka left by the retreating Germans when they were forced out by the Americans in January 1945.

A British soldier outfitted in a white snowsuit, poses with his Projector, Infantry, Anti Tank (PIAT) weapon in an open field somewhere in Belgium.

American troops examine an ammunition container dropped by German aircraft for their paratroopers that were part of the early phases of the Ardennes Offensive. The container has grenades, machine gun ammunition boxes and panzerfaust rounds.

Two American soldiers inspect a pile of captured German weapons that includes a bunch of rifles and two panzerfaust anti-tank weapons.

Captain William Talbot of the 324th Combat Engineer Battalion of the 99th Infantry Division instructs soldiers on the use of a flamethrower at the beginning of the Battle of the Bulge.

Near Hotton, Belgium on December 28, 1944, T/5 Henry Koller of the 23rd Armored Engineer Battalion lays mines on the shoulders of the road should the German forces in the area breakthrough the lines.

Engineer with the 51st Combat Engineer Battalion lays mines in a daisy chain formation to be pulled across the road if enemy vehicles breakthrough near Marche, Belgium.

Also with the 51st Combat Engineer Battalion near March, Belgium, an engineer prepares to blow up TNT charges on trees to make a roadblock against the enemy.

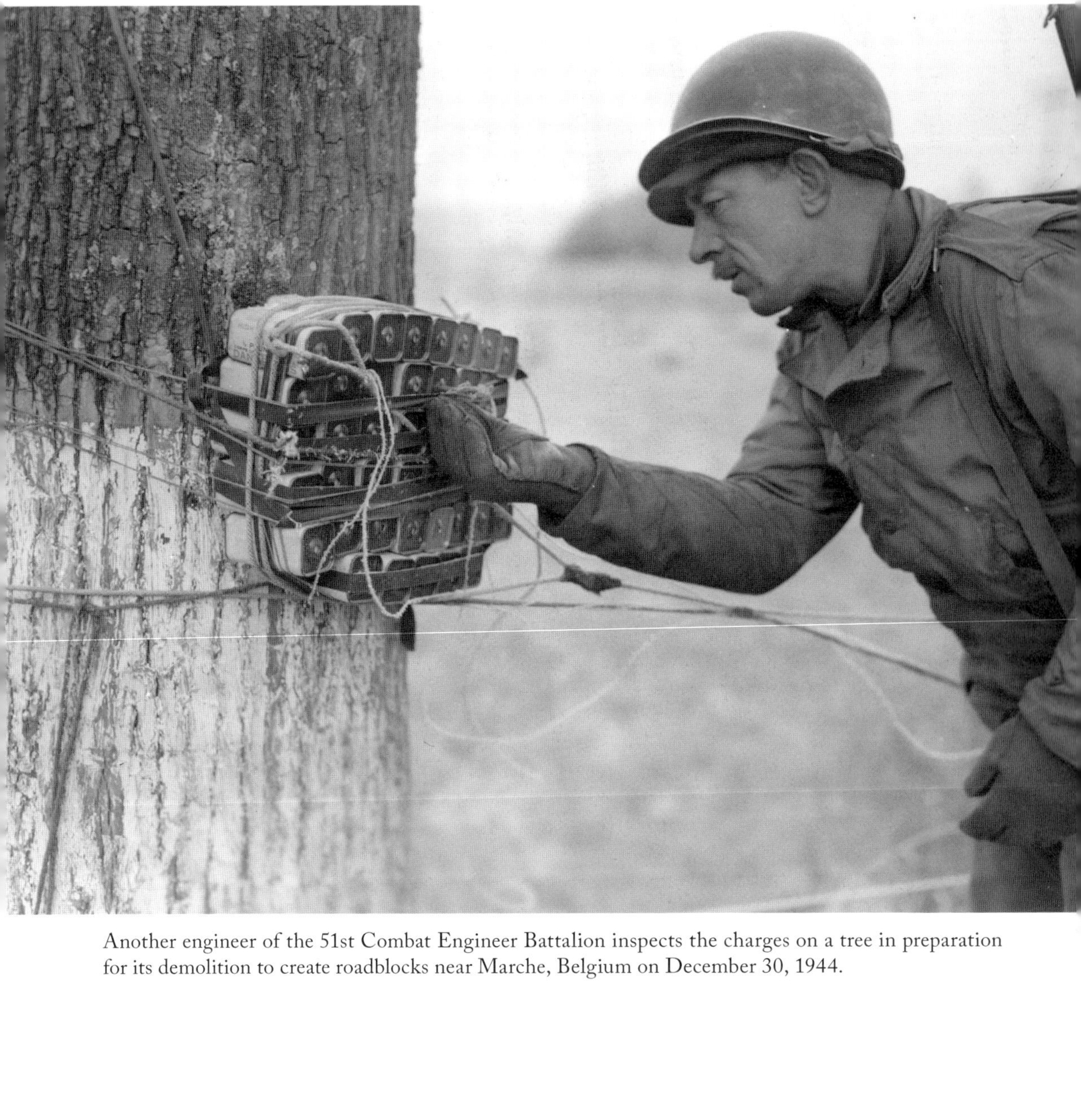

Another engineer of the 51st Combat Engineer Battalion inspects the charges on a tree in preparation for its demolition to create roadblocks near Marche, Belgium on December 30, 1944.

An American soldier inspects captured German mines and panzerfausts after the Germans had retreated in this part of the Ardennes.

Soldiers of the 6th Armored Division in Kalborn, Luxembourg inspect a German Sd. Kfz 251/17 with a 20mm Schwebelafette, but with the gun missing. However, the photograph provides a good detail of the shield around the gun.

A M45 quadmount on a trailer being checked out by a curious German soldier during the initial German breakthrough at the beginning of the Bulge. This weapon belongs to the 413th AAA Battalion and based on the swastika markings on the quadmount, has claimed credit for 4 enemy aircraft destroyed.

An American soldier aims his 40mm anti-aircraft gun towards the sky while looking for enemy aircraft.

A soldier assigned to the 30th Infantry Division near Malmedy, Belgium on December 22, 1944 mans a .50 caliber M45 quadmount weapon system for an anti-infantry role. According to the official signal corps caption, four of these weapons broke up a major infantry attack the night before.

A two man crew of a M45 quadmount weapon system scans the sky for enemy aircraft during the early days of the Battle of the Bulge.

A M45 quadmount is moved to a truck for transportation to be mounted on a trailer for use in the Battle of the Bulge.

Two soldiers with the 460th AAA Battalion, attached to the 30th Infantry Division near Stavelot, Belgium stand on duty with their .50 caliber quadmount for enemy action on January 2, 1945.

When attached to a M17 trailer as seen in this photo, the M45 quadmount was known as the M51 gun system. Here a unit scans the sky for enemy aircraft outside Bastogne, Belgium on January 11, 1945.

A lone soldier mans a M45 quadmount in the middle of a snowy field somewhere in Belgium in January 1945.

An American soldier inspects a German mortar left by elements of Kampfgruppe Peiper in La Gleize, Belgium. In addition to numerous tanks and armored vehicles, the Germans left behind several heavy weapons.

American infantrymen with the 83rd Infantry Division fire a 60mm mortar in Malempre, Belgium to batter dug-in Germans on the edge of town on January 6, 1945.

Two soldiers with the 334th Infantry, 84th Infantry Division dig an emplacement for their 81mm mortar near Samree, Belgium in January 1945.

In the snowy woods around Bovigny, Belgium, two soldiers of Company H, 329th Infantry Regiment, 83rd Infantry Division set up a 81mm mortar position.

Sergeant Eldred Wallingford of the 87th Chemical Mortar Battalion sets sights for a smoke bombardment near Berismenil, Belgium on January 14, 1945.

Near Bovigny, Belgium, Corporal Dean Herod with the 87th Chemical Mortar Battalion elevates his mortar to a firing position in support of attacking troops on January 17, 1945.

A member of a 81mm mortar crew awaits firing orders from the command post near Schoppen, Belgium on January 22, 1945. Notice all the rounds stacked and ready to be fired.

Covering a bridge in the 82nd Airborne area near Habiemont, Belgium in late December 1944, a solder mans an 40mm anti-aircraft gun.

While enjoying a light moment on skis, a soldier with the 230th Field Artillery Battalion, 30th Infantry Division almost runs into a 40mm anti-aircraft gun position in Belgium on December 31, 1944.

Anti-aircraft gun crew attached to the 30th Infantry Division shares a lighthearted moment for the cameraman in Stavelot, Belgium on January 6, 1945. The 40mm gun has the name "destroyer" painted on it.

Tanks of the 4th Armored Division near Sainlex, Belgium pass by a dead and frozen German soldier alongside his 2cm Flakvierling 38. This four barrel weapon was also used in the ground role when needed and could wreak havoc.

Two GIs examine a knocked out 40mm anti-aircraft gun outside Bastogne on January 2, 1945. The weapon is missing two tires from one side, possibly taken by civilians for their personal use.

A GI from the 3rd Army in Tarchamps, Luxembourg inspects a 6 barrel 15 cm Nebelwerfer 41 rocket launcher. The six tube launcher was mounted on a towed carriage and had a range of up to 7,500 yds.

Another 3rd Army soldier in Luxembourg looks down the front of a 5 barrel 21 cm Nebelwerfer 42 rocket launcher. The photograph caption noted that dynamite had been placed in the barrels by retreating Germans to blow it up to prevent its use by American troops but the retreat was so sudden that they didn't have time to destroy it.

A 57mm anti-tank gun crew struggles in the mud to move their weapon to a position to prepare to repel the German armor advance near Butgenbach, Belgium in December 1944. The soldiers are with the 1st Battalion, 26th Infantry, 1st Infantry Division.

An American towed 3-inch antiitank gun lays destroyed outside the town of Humain, Belgium on December 28, 1944. These 3-inch guns were the primary weapons of the towed tank destroyer units.

Outside Amonines, Belgium a gun crew of a 30inch antiitank gun guards a minefield. The gun is part of the antiitank platoon of HQ company, 2nd Battalion, 335th Infantry, 84th Infantry Division on January 4, 1945.

In the midst of deep snow and frigid conditions, an American anti-tank gun crew moves their gun into position to prepare for any German armor in their area.

An American 155mm howitzer fires in support of infantry somewhere in the Ardennes battles in late December 1944.

A 155mm howitzer gun crew of the 254th Field Artillery Battalion attached to the 82nd Airborne in Werbomont, Belgium stands by for firing orders. The snow that fell on the netting has provided an excellent natural camouflage for the crew.

Near Malmedy, Belgium on January 2, 1945, Sgt Pete Bludie with Battery C, 230th Field Artillery scans the front for enemy action. His 105mm howitzer stands by for infantry support or to break up any German attack.

An unidentified unit of the First Army digs in next to their howitzer in the frozen ground of Belgium during the Bulge. Once the emplacement was dug out, the artillery piece would be moved in to a firing position.

One of the more famous photos of the Battle of the Bulge. A knocked out 105mm howitzer lies on the roadside somewhere in the 3rd Armored Division sector of Belgium.

Members of Battery B, 376th Parachute Field Artillery, 82nd Airborne prepare to fire their 75mm pack howitzer towards the enemy across the Salm River on January 9, 1945. The pack howitzer was designed to be moved across difficult terrain, and the gun and carriage could be broken down into several pieces.

A nice close up view of the 75mm pack howitzer as a soldier sets his target and prepares to fire.

Gun crew from Battery B, 266th Field Artillery Battalion guard a road near Verieumont, Belgium on January 13, 1945.

An artilleryman makes good use of a sheet "found" from a local Belgian home to camouflage his artillery piece somewhere in the VII Corps sector of Belgium in January 1945.

Artillery unit attached to the 26th Infantry Division aim and prepare to load their 105 mm Howitzer M3 in support of attacking infantry troops in January 1945 in Luxembourg.

A wide shot of guns from the same unit pictured previously in firing action.

Soldier with Cannon Company, 329th Infantry Regiment, 83rd Infantry Diviion applies white sheets for camouflage to his 105mm howitzer outside of Houffalize, Belgium on January 9, 1945. A gun from his unit can also be seen in the background next to a tree.

Pfc Clifford Tibbets of an anti-tank company of the 331st Infantry, 83rd Infantry Division also used white sheets to camouflage his 57mm anti-tank gun near a large pile of straw outside Langlir, Belgium on January 14, 1945.

Crew of an American 57mm anti-tank gun guard a snow covered road with tall trees on either side. They are on guard for any German armor that may try and breakthrough the lines here.

American soldiers of the 1st Infantry Division tow their 57mm anti-tank gun through Steinbach, Belgium on January 21, 1945. The jeep to the left was knocked out by a German mine earlier.

This soldier of the 83rd Infantry Division awoke to an overnight snowstorm that has covered his 57mm anti-tank gun. He will need to clean it off and check all the mechanisms to ensure its ready for action.

The 90mm anti-aircraft gun was used frequently in the anti-tank role and here one is set up in Belgium near Malmedy in the early days of the Ardennes Offensive. This gun is guarding an important road junction.

Another 90mm anti-aircraft gun being deployed in the anti-armor role somewhere in the 30th Infantry Division sector in the early days of the Bulge.

Soldier of a field artillery unit uses his bayonet to open containers of 105mm shells near his battery's firing position somewhere in Belgium.

Pfc Patrick Mccarthy prepares a 105mm shell for firing. He is with Battery A, 7th Field Artillery Battalion, 1st Infantry Division.

A 155mm gun crew prepares to load a shell with a special New Year's message for Hitler. Based on the patch of the soldier on the right, they are with a field artillery unit of the First Army.

Artilleryman of the 195th Field Artillery Battalion scrapes snow from 8-inch shells while other members of the crew prepare their gun for action near Freyneux, Belgium on January 9, 1945.

A close-up of the same gun in the previous photo. Crew members emplace the 8-inch gun in preparation for firing towards the German lines in Freyneux, Belgium.

GIs with a Cannon company of the 84th Infantry Division prepare their 105mm howitzer for action near Odeigne, Belgium on January 11, 1945.

The immense size of the 8-inch howitzer can be seen in this photo in addition to the size of the gun crew needed to fire it. This gun is from the 578th Field Artillery Battalion of the 90th Infantry Division and is named "Big Mama".

A 240mm howitzer prepares to fire in the Houffalize sector of Belgium on January 13, 1945.

Crew members of the 266th Field Artillery Battalion, places powder bags in the breech of the tube of a 240mm howitzer near Verieumont, Belgium on January 13, 1945.

Men from the same gun crew in the previous photo carry the large shell for the 240mm gun in preparation for firing.

Artillery tractor pulls an 8-inch howitzer down a snowy road during the height of the snow storms during the Battle of the Bulge. What appears to be whitewash on the artillery piece is actually snow.

155mm shells for the M-12 self propelled gun receive fuses as a soldier readies them for firing by his unit near Ottre, Belgium on January 14, 1945. The unit is the 991st Field Artillery Battalion, serving with the 3rd Armored Division at the time.

Soldiers take ammunition from a straw shelter where it was being kept dry to prepare their 105mm howitzer for firing. The soldiers are with the 325th Field Artillery Battalion of the 84th Infantry Division.

Due to the Americans' shortage of 105mm howitzers during the Bulge, the British supplied them with 25 pounder howitzers. Here, an American crew from the 195th Field Artillery Battalion receives firing instruction from a British soldier.

The next two photos are of destroyed American 105mm howitzers of the 35th Infantry Division somewhere in Luxembourg.

American soldier takes a closer look at one of the abandoned 105mm guns, this one named "Bloody Yank" on the gunshield.

An American soldier stands guard by a captured German artillery piece outside of La Gleize, Belgium after Kampfgruppe Peiper was pushed out of that village.

American troops prepare to pull a German anti-tank gun with an artillery tractor in Luxembourg after the retreat of the Germans in that area.

First Army troops inspect an abandoned German 10 cm schwere Kanone 18 in Belgium during the early days of the Ardennes Offensive.

A German 88mm anti-aircraft gun sits captured with other artillery pieces in Ciney, Belgium on December 27, 1944.

Also in the same location as the captured 88mm in the previous photograph were these two 15 cm schwere Feldhaubitze 18s. They still have their tree branch foliage camouflage attached to them. The location is Ciney, Belgium, December 27, 1944.

Near Hubaille, Belgium in the 2nd Armored Division sector, this German 88mm gun was captured in the woods. The caption stated it was part a German 2nd Panzer Division convoy surprised by the Americans.

Also nearby the 88mm gun pictured previously was this German 3.7cm Flak 43 weapon. Location is Hubaille, Belgium and the American unit closest was CCB of the 2nd Armored Division.

Men of the 578th Field Artillery Battalion, 90th Infantry Division prepare to fire a captured German 88mm gun back towards the German lines somewhere in Luxembourg, January 11, 1945.

A 3-inch anti-tank gun of the 823rd Tank Destroyer Battalion (towed) is covered in whitewash and white sheets and stands guard near Hedomont, Belgium on January 14, 1945.

A captured German artillery position outside La Gleize, Belgium in January 1945. This photograph shows the detail of the landscape in this area, wooded ridges with deep valleys.

American soldiers with the 83rd Infantry Division inspect a German howitzer in Belgium after the Germans had retreated in their sector.

A German 105mm howitzer sits covered in snow after being abandoned outside Bastogne on January 19, 1945 and captured by troops of the 6th Armored Division.

A German 75mm anti-tank gun sits looking towards its prey, an American M3 half-track near Wardin, Belgium.

A captured German 75mm anti-tank gun sits alone with open ammunition boxes littered around it somewhere in a snowy field in Belgium. This was a common sight as the German offensive was pushed back and they retreated.

A soldier with Battery B, 5th Field Artillery Battalion, 1st Infantry Division inspects a German 37mm anti-tank gun on a snowy roadside near Muringen, Belgium on January 30, 1945 after the Ardennes battles were over.

Chapter 3

Armored Fighting Vehicles (AFVs)

When reading and imagining the Battle of the Bulge, we think of American tanks racing to the encircled paratroopers at Bastogne and massive German Tiger tanks trying to maneuver narrow snowy roads in the Ardennes. The snowy conditions caused the Americans to rush to implement whitewashing of their armored vehicles and the installation of duck-bill extenders for their tank tracks to help move in the deep snow. Thousands of armored vehicles were thrown into battle by both sides from armored cars, halftracks, self-propelled artillery and anti-tank guns to the light and medium tanks used by the Americans to the standard German Panzer IV, Panther and the feared Tiger II.

German tank units were typically from their panzer divisions, while the Americans in addition to their armored divisions had independent tank battalions of about 68-70 tanks that were assigned to an infantry division for support. In addition, they had tank destroyer battalions of about 36 tank destroyers that could be called on for divisional support as well. As with other parts of the war, while some of the German tanks were superior to their American counterparts, especially in terms of main tank guns, the Americans simply had more of them. So while the American units were suffering high tank losses, especially in the beginning of the campaign, they were able to replace them, usually within 24 hours. Task Force Lovelady of the 3rd Armored Division lost almost all their medium tanks one day in mid-January 1945 and within 36 hours were back up to full strength. The Germans did not have this luxury and they also faced fuel shortages and basic mechanical support. Many of the photographs of German tanks that follow were a case of empty gas tanks and breakdowns and not put out of action by the American forces. As the Germans retreated to their border near the end of January, and also when the clear skies opened up, German tanks were easy targets for Allied fighter bombers.

Knocked out tanks were always of interest to the signal corps cameramen, thus this chapter is almost two-and-a-half times as large as the infantry and support weapons chapters. In many of the photos you will see the cameramen themselves or members of their photo team showing where rounds penetrated armor, ripped off tracks or blew off the entire turret. American technical ordnance soldiers also photographed many of these vehicles for analytical reports before shipping them off to the states for further evaluation. Some of these vehicles, like the famous Tiger

332 is still available for viewing at the US Armor Museum at Fort Benning in the United States.

The following chapter starts with armored cars and then moves to halftracks. Those are followed by tank destroyers and other self-propelled guns. American light and medium tanks follow that and the chapter concludes with German tanks. There are far superior literary works to consult for the reader that wants to learn more about the technical intricacies and model types of the vehicles that follow. This chapter is not meant to be a technical study but rather a pictorial history of those AFVs used by both sides, in extremely large quantities in this campaign that was fought in conditions of snow and ice that presented the armored crews with another threat and foe.

American troops stand guard on the edge of a forest in the Ardennes with their heavily camouflaged M20 Armored Car.

A M8 Armored Car of the 90th Infantry Division stands guard over a field in Luxembourg in January 1945.

Using a whitewash mix, men of the 4th Infantry Division paint their M8 Armored car behind the front lines on January 14, 1945.

Halftrack of the 3rd Armored Division pulls a M8 Armored Car back onto the road after icy conditions caused it to slip off the road onto the embankment, Belgium, January 16, 1945.

GIs of the 84th Infantry Division greet a driver of M8 Armored Car signifying the meet up of the First and Third Armies in January 1945 and bringing the majority of the Bulge actions to a close. The armored car has had a coat of whitewash applied to it.

A great side view of a M8 Armored Car from the 4th Cavalry Squadron around Borzee, Belgium on January 16, 1945. The armored car shows remnant of a whitewash application and also has chains installed on its tires for traction control.

A M20 Armored Car of CCB, 10th Armored Division is seen near Metz, France after having been pulled back from the Bastogne sector of operations on January 17, 1945.

Krinkelt, Belgium was the scene of fierce fighting during the Ardennes battles. Here a M8 Armored Car with the name "Sprocket" painted on and First Army markings sits knocked out in the village of Krinkelt.

Men of a M8 Armored perform maintenance of their vehicle near Wilwerwiltz, Luxembourg after the Bulge battles had ended. The men are with A Troop, 6th Cavalry Reconnaissance Squadron.

Soldier from the 6th Armored Division inspects an overturned M8 Armored Car that had been captured by the Germans and put to use before being knocked out. The location of this is around Neffe, Belgium in January 1945.

Amongst a plethora of captured German vehicles and weapons, an American soldier stands on a German Sd.Kfz.233 near Celles, Belgium in late December 1944. The vehicles would have been part of Pz.AA.2 of the 2nd Panzer Division.

At the same collection point as the previous photo, a GI checks out the engine of a German Sd.Kfz.261 armored car. In the background are additional vehicles and weapons.

This photograph is also from the collection point near Celles and shows two German 15cm SIG33 guns sitting near a German Sd.Kfz. 234/2 armored car that has a flat rear tire.

A British soldier takes a closer look at one of the German Sd.Kfz.233 captured from the 2nd Panzer Division near Celles.

In the early confusing days of the Battle of the Bulge, everyone was being questioned. Here an American jeep passing a column of trucks is being questioned by military policemen in Belgium, December 1944.

Medics of the 32nd Armored Regiment, 3rd Armored Division check out their jeep knocked out by German artillery fire in Sadzot, Belgium late December 1944. The red cross markings on the jeep didn't save it from enemy fire this time.

According to the official signal corps caption, this dog sitting in a knocked out American jeep in Langlir, Belgium belonged to a German soldier that had been killed in the area.

An American jeep of the 4th Cavalry Reconnaissance Squadron and armed with a .30 caliber machine gun passes the frozen bodies of both German and American soldiers on the outskirts of La Roche, Belgium on January 12, 1945.

Just a few weeks after Kampfgruppe Peiper left the town of La Gleize, the 82nd Airborne had elements in the town. Here we see heavily armored and whitewashed jeeps of the 82nd preparing for patrol around the town on January 18, 1945.

Another photo taken in the same sequence shows the immense size of the .50 caliber machine gun as compared to the jeep. The driver has a thin slit for visibility. The engine grill even has an armored plate installed to protect it.

Official Signal Corps cameraman George Meyer examines an American jeep that was a victim of German mines in the Longvilly area of Belgium in January 1945.

An American M4 medium tank of the 2nd Armored Division stands guard at a roadblock near Amonines, Belgium on January 4, 1945. Behind it sits an abandoned German Kubelwagen.

An American soldier looks at wrecked German trucks that were part of a convoy of the 2nd Panzer Division and were knocked out by Combat Command B (CCB) of the 2nd Armored Division in the woods near Hubaille, Belgium in late December 1944.

An MP marches German prisoners down a road as an American halftrack from the 10th Armored Infantry Battalion, 4th Armored Division passes them by. The half-track is armored with a .30 caliber water cooled machine gun.

A disabled American halftrack named "Agnes IV" from the 9th Armored Division sits on a road on the outskirts of Sibret, Belgium. This vehicles was equipped with a .50 caliber machine gun.

A M15A1 anti-aircraft halftrack of the 197th AAA Battalion stands guard on a wrecked bridge in Limbourg, Belgium on December 29, 1944. The M15A1 consisted of a single 40mm gun and twin .50 caliber machine guns that were situated on either side of the 40mm.

An American M3A1 halftrack that was captured by the Germans sits abandoned in a ditch outside of Neufchateau and Bastogne on December 29, 1944.

An American halftrack sits knocked out after a German artillery bombardment in the city square of Bastogne. Based on the CCB markings on the bumper, it is probably from the 9th Armored Division.

Men of the 777th AAA Battalion and 101st Airborne Division warm themselves in front of halftrack. over a small fire on the outskirts of Bastogne on December 31, 1944.

Camouflaged M5A1 light tank and M3A1 halftrack sit side by side for comparison in a snow covered area in Heffingen, Luxembourg on January 6, 1945. The halftrack has chains on the tires and tow bar on the hood, 737th Tank Battalion and 5th Infantry Division.

Halftrack of the 83rd Infantry Division leads a column of vehicles through Lierneux, Belgium in January 1945.

A M45 quadmount system on this halftrack would make it a M16 Gun Motor Carriage. This vehicle guards a bridge in the rear that has been repaired by American engineers.

In Cherain, Belgium, an American medical halftrack of the 3rd Armored Division picks up wounded soldiers for transport to a field hospital. Medium tanks of the 3rd Armored can be seen in the background.

A soldier with the 15th Tank Battalion, 6th Armored Division places boxes of ammunition on the side of his halftrack somewhere in Belgium, January 1945.

An M3 halftrack of the 52nd Armored Infantry of the 9th Armored that was captured by the Germans and put to their use until being knocked out around Lullange, Luxembourg. German crosses have been painted on the sides and rear of the vehicle.

An M-25 tank retriever (dragon wagon) pulls an overturned tank destroyer that can't be seen in this photo from the 702nd Tank Destroyer Battalion that had skidded off a road and overturned, killing some of the crew near Fisennes, Belgium on January 3, 1945.

M-29 cargo carrier "Weasel" in a nice winter camouflage paint scheme carries wounded soldiers in Belgium.

Another M-29 weasel cargo carrier with winter camouflage applied is moved off a 2 ½ ton truck for use with the 83rd Infantry Division around Petit Langlir in January 1945.

A captured German Sd.Kfz. 251/9 "Stummel" halftrack painted with American stars sits in a farmyard after its captured by elements of the 82nd Airborne Division in the early stages of the Battle of the Bulge.

GIs of the 3rd Armored Division look over the remains of a German Sd.Kfz 251 halftrack with its engine compartment blown off in Hotton, Belgium. In the rear a German Panzer IV can be seen as well.

In an orchard in La Gleize, Belgium sit at least 7 different German Sd.kfz 251s from Kampfgruppe Peiper that were abandoned when he and his unit retreated from the area.

US soldier from 702nd Tank Battalion whose tank knocked out one German tank and four halftracks looks at a knocked out German Sd.kfz 251/17 that has been equipped with a 2cm autocannon.

Outsisde of Buissonville, Belgium, men from the 2nd Armored Division examine a German Sd.kfz.7 prime mover that has been destroyed by American firepower.

American vehicle rolls past an abandoned German Sd.Kfz. 250/3 halftrack from the 2nd Panzer Division near Buissonville, Belgium on January 2, 1945.

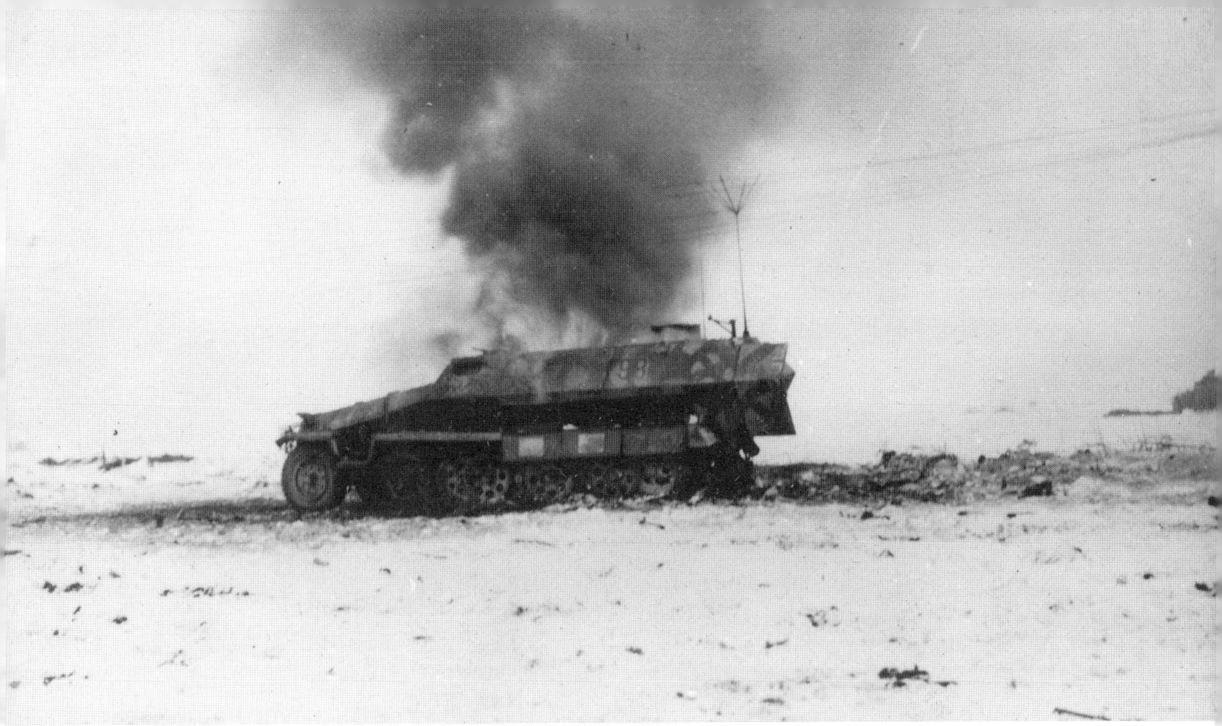

Outside Jodenville, Belgium on January 6, 1945, the 56th Armored Engineer Battalion of the 11th Armored Division set afire this German Sd.Kfz 251/6 command post halftrack.

A GI inspects a captured German Sd.Kfz 251 halftrack near Marcourt on January 13, 1945. The German crew has equipped the halftrack with a .50 caliber machine gun instead of the normal MG42.

American soldiers with the 16th Infantry, 1st Infantry Division have put a captured German Sd.Kfz 251/7 engineer halftrack to their use in Schoppen, Belgium on January 22, 1945. A large white star has been painted on the back to avoid any confusion to friendly troops.

Two photos of the same scene in Amel, Belgium on January 24, 1945. As the Germans retreated the Americans found numerous loads of weapons, vehicles and other equipment left behind. Here a soldier with the 1st Infantry Division inspects a rubber raft and its inflater mechanism to the rear of German Sd.Kfz. 251.7 engineer halftrack.

A knocked out M4 medium tank of the 6th Armored Division sits near an abandoned German Sd.Kfz. 251 that was being used in the ambulance role. The original caption said the tank was knocked out by bazooka fire from enemy troops in the church and the halftrack. The scene is Wardin, Belgium on January 17, 1945.

A German Sd.Kfz. 251/21, armed with a triple Drilling MG151S was captured by 6th Armored Division soldiers near Kalborn, Luxembourg near the German border. It is missing the usual armored shield around the gun mount.

American soldiers walk past at least three knocked out German halftracks with more vehicles in the rear in the town of Samree Belgium in January 1945.

American tankers install duck-bill track extenders on their M4A1 medium (76) medium tank while a German Sd.Kfz 251/9 "Stummel" sits snow covered outside the hamlet of Ster, Belgium. These German vehicles were armed with a 7.5 cm cannon and were quite powerful.

German Sd.Kfz 7 primer movers sit wrecked and snow covered in a field outside of a farmhouse somewhere in Luxembourg after the Germans retreated in this area in January 1945.

The Germans pressed this ex-Italian SPA TL37 artillery tractor into service. This photo was taken somewhere in the area between Tarchamps and Watrange, Luxembourg in January 1945.

A German Sd.Kfz. 251/3 previously thought to be from Panzer Lehr Division is most likely from the Fuhrer Begleit Brigade and lost somewhere in Luxembourg in the 26th Infantry Division sector.

A German Daimler-Benz DB 12 ton Zugkraftwagen probably of the 2nd Panzer Division lies disabled in the streets of Marnach, Luxembourg in January 25, 1945.

These two photos are taken from a report simply called the "Howell Mission" to the Ardennes area after the battles. The first photo is a Sd.Kfz. 11/1 that would have been armed with a 2cm Flak 38. The next photo and heavily covered in snow is a German Sd.Kfz.251/9 "Stummel".

An American soldier from the Third Army inspects a captured German Sd.Kfz. 251/17 armed with a 2cm autocannon. This particular vehicle was part of an ETO technical evaluation report.

A badly shot up German Sd.Kfz 11. The front left tire has been knocked off the rim and the vehicle still carries brush that had provided effective camouflage. This particular vehicle was 3 ton halftrack that shared a chassis similar to that of the Sd.Kfz. 251 series and was used as a tractor for many types of weapons.

A German Raupenschlepper Ost "Caterpillar Tractor East" or RSO. The RSO was a fully tracked, lightweight vehicle used to tow weapons and maneuver on adverse ground conditions.

In Marnach, Lxuembourg, an American paratrooper with the 17th Airborne Division lays communication wire to his artillery observation post. In the rear is a knocked out German Sd.Kfz. 251 that has had its front wheels removed and damage to the engine compartment.

Crew of an M7 105mm howitzer motor carriage (HMC) loads a shell for a fire mission in Luxembourg in the early days of the Battle of the Bulge.

An M7 105mm HMC of the 7th Armored Division under camouflage netting cleans and open shells for their gun while in position along the highway near Manhay, Belgium on December 27, 1944.

Soldiers of the 101st Airborne walk past an M8 75mm HMC draped with a white sheet for extra camouflage protection outside of Bastogne on December 26, 1944.

Nice frontal view of "C-12", an M7 105MM HMC of an unknown armored field artillery battalion somewhere in Belgium during the Battle of the Bulge.

Crew members of an M12 155mm Gun Motor Carriage (GMC) share a smoke in between fire missions. Their M12 has a netting draped over the top for camouflage and part of the name can be seen on the side, "Warrior".

Crew of a M7 105mm HMC scramble to their vehicle for a fire mission near Oster, Belgium on January 7, 1945. This M7 is adorned with brush and branches for camouflage and also a tarp over top for protection from the winter elements. The M7 is with the 87th Armored Field Artillery Battalion.

An M7 105 HMC is pulled back onto the road by a tow truck to the right of the vehicle. No location or unit was provided in the caption but the area is typical of the Ardennes region and the weather suggests sometime in January of 1945.

A soldier of the 84th Infantry Division inspects an abandoned M7 105 HMC in Marcouray, Belgium on January 10, 1945. The vehicle is from Battery C of the 54th Armored Field Artillery Battalion, 3rd Armored Division and was left behind by Task Force Hogan before they returned to lines by foot. The M7 is a veteran of the Normandy campaigns as it has hedgerow cutters applied to the frontal bow armor.

M7 105mm HMC of the 212th Armored Field Artillery Battalion, 6th Armored Division sits under a snow covered camouflage netting and waits for its next fire mission outside Bastogne on January 8, 1945.

A crew of a M7 105 HMC has some fun with an umbrella for the cameraman near Morhet, Belgium on January 9, 1945. The M7 is with the 492nd Armored Field Artillery Battalion of the 11th Armored Division. Note the neatly stacked spent shell casings.

With stacks of shells surrounding it, this M7 105mm HMC named "Acrobat III" prepares to fire against enemy troops somewhere in Belgium in January 1945. This view shows how exposed the crew was to the elements when not covered with a tarp.

A M12 155mm GMC attached to the 3rd Armored Division is receiving a shell for firing towards the German lines near Ottre, Belgium on January 14, 1945. This gun is being manned by a crew of six artillerymen.

A knocked out M7 105mm HMC sits on the roadside near Longvilly, Belgium in late January 1945. No unit was provided in the caption.

An interior view of the vehicle previously shown. This view provides great detail of the howitzer and its firing mechanisms and also of spare shells stacked on the left side for easy and quick access.

Artillerymen of the 400th Armored Field Artillery Battalion warm themselves around a fire near their M7 105mm HMC from Battery B. To the rear of the men a wooded dugout has been constructed for warmth and shelter.

Outside La Gleize, Belgium, a crew of a M12 155mm GMC prepares their shells and gun for a fire mission. This gun belonged to the 987th Field Artillery Battalion. The M12 has large hoops over it for placement of camouflage netting.

This German Sd.Kfz.138/1 "Grille" of the 1st SS Panzer Division, Kampfgruppe Peiper was one of six vehicles of the same type left by the Germans when they retreated from La Gleize, Belgium.

Near La Gleize, the signal corps cameraman who took the previous photo stopped near Stoumont and the Sanatorium St-Edouard and photographed this German Wirbelwind anti-aircraft gun of the 1st SS Panzer Division. The vehicle was put out of action by the 119th Infantry Regiment, 30th Infantry Division.

German 170mm self-propelled gun "Hummel" was left behind in Kalborn, Luxembourg during Allied air attacks as the Germans retreated over the Our River to Germany in late January 1945. There appears to be no signs of battle damage leading to the assumption that is simply abandoned by the retreating Germans.

Another abandoned German Flappzner IV "wirbelwind" anti-aircraft gun sits snow covered on a roadside in Belgium, January 27, 1945. In addition to the snow that is covering it, communications teams have been draping signal wire on it as well.

An M36 90mm GMC of the 703rd Tank Destroyer Battalion moves up to the front to meet the attacking Germans during the first few days of the Ardennes Offensive.

An M10 3-inch GMC of a tank destroyer battalion in the First Army sector moves down a road towards the front to blunt the German attacks.

In the 7th Armored Division sector near Manhay, a M36 90mm GMC of the 814th Tank Destroyer Battalion scans the front for enemy movement. This M36 has been placed into a firing pit that has been dug out by engineers.

A m36 90mm GMC of the 628th Tank Destroyer Battalion with camouflage added to break up its profile, stands guard near a position looking over the L'Ourthe River valley in Hotton, Belgium on December 30, 1944.

Soldier in a snowsuit stands near a M36 90mm GMC to show the effectiveness of white camouflage in the snowy conditions at the height of the Battle of the Bulge.

On January 5, 1945 a M36 90mm GMC of the 703rd Tank Destroyer Battalion, 3rd Armored Division moves up towards Malempre, Belgium as the Americans begin their counterattack after the initial limited success of the Germans in December 1944.

Series of 6 photos that show the aftermath of a M36 90mm GMC of the 702nd Tank Destroyer Battalion that overturned when it slipped off an embankment near Fisennes, Belgium in early January 1945.

This photo shows the M36 after it had overturned when it skidded off the embankment.

Rear view of the vehicle as onlookers review what happened and prepare to get the vehicle overturned.

Cables have been attached from an M25 recovery vehicles and the man in the foreground instructs the crew to begin pulling the M36 over.

The M36 completes its recovery process.

Now that the vehicle has been uprighted, soldiers tend to the crew members that were killed in the incident.

Medical personnel remove the casualties from the scene while another soldier checks to see if the M36 is still serviceable.

An M36 90mm GMC of the 703rd Tank Destroyer Battalion, 3rd Armored has found itself stuck in mud near Manhay, Belgium on January 4, 1945.

Another photo of the same M36, this time from the front and showing how far the front of the tank destroyer has sunk into the mud.

Crew of a M10 3-inch GMC of the 629th Tank Destroyer Battalion tries to stay warm around a fire in front of their vehicle near Manhay, Belgium on January 4, 1945. This unit was in action days earlier against German tanks of the 2nd Ss Panzer Division.

A wrecked M10 3-inch GMC of the 654th Tank Destroyer Battalion supporting the 35th Infantry Division at the time sits after being knocked out by German mines in the Livarchamps region SE of Bastogne on January 6, 1945.

A newly arrived M18 76mm GMC of the 638th Tank Destroyer Battalion supporting the 84th Infantry Division sits in Marcouray, Belgium on January 10, 1945. The 638th received 5 new M18s in earl January and according to the after-action reports on January 9 claimed to have knocked out 3 German tanks and 1 SP gun.

Crew of a M36 90mm GMC of the 702nd Tank Destroyer Battalion, 2nd Armored Division change their steel tracks to rubber for better traction. The location of this photograph is Dochamps, Belgium on January 10, 1945.

An M10 3-inch GMC of the 773rd Tank Destroyer Battalion attached to the 90th Infantry Division stands guard over a field NE of Bavigne, Luxembourg on January 10, 1945.

Another M10 of the 773nd Tank Destroyer Battalion rolls down the road in Berle, Luxembourg during the 90th Infantry Division's push on the German southern flank in this area. The damage to the town during the battles is quite evident from this photograph.

This M10 3-inch GMC of Company B, 629th Tank Destroyer Battalion was credited with knocking out two German Panzer IV tanks shortly before this photograph was taken near Bovigny, Belgium on January 16, 1945.

M36 90mm GMC of the 702nd Tank Destroyer Battalion with medium tanks from the 2nd Armored Division in the background move around Houffalizer, Belgium.

A GI follows a M10 3-inch GMC of the 629th Tank Destroyer Battalion through the snowy streets of Bovigny past a World War I memorial outside a church on January 20, 1945.

Another photo of a 629th Tank Destroyer crew in the snowy woods of Belgium near the end of the Bulge battles. Here men from Company C warm themselves over a fire.

An M36 90mm GMC streams past an ambulance as the armor of CCA, 7th Armored Division moves towards the front near Weims, Belgium on January 20, 1945.

Men of 773rd Tank Destroyer Battalion pass near Benonchamps Luxembourg. This crew and their M10 3-inch GMC knocked out five German tanks near Oberwampach, Luxembourg.

A crew from an US Army Air Force bomber meets the crew of a M10 3-inch GMC of the 1st Infantry Division in Schoppen, Belgium on January 23, 1945. The purpose of the visit to was to gain a better understanding of ground forces and their operations.

A whitewashed M18 76mm GMC assigned to the 612th Tank Destroyer Battalion lays down indirect fire on German positions in support of the 2nd Infantry Division near Nidrum, Belgium on January 25, 1945.

In the town of Esch-Sur-la-Sure in Luxembourg in late January 1945, crews of the 818th Tank Destroyer Battalion whitewash their M10 3-inch GMCs in the town square. The unit was supporting the 26th Infantry Division at the time. Both M10s still have hedgerow cutters applied to them.

A knocked out American M18 76mm GMC sits in a field in the Bastogne sector in January 1945. No unit identification is available for this vehicle.

Series of 3 phots showing soldiers and a bulldozer from the 35th Combat Engineer Battalion removing a pair of Jagdpanzer 38(t) from the road in Belgium after the Bulge battles had ended.

Two photos of the same German Sturmgeschutz III from H.St.Art.Brig.911 attached to the Fuhrer-Grenadier Brigade. The right side track and running gear has been damaged. This photo was most likely taken in Luxembourg in the 26th Infantry Division sector.

A much clearer view of the right side of the same Stug III and now just visible under the snow on the front is a layer of concrete applied over the front of the fighting compartment.

A German Panzer IV/70(V) of the Fuhrer Grenadier Brigade lays knocked out roadside in Luxembourg in January 1945. Interesting that this vehicle has a threaded end to gun barrel for a muzzle brake that was never fitted.

Other side view of the same Jagdpanzer IV/70(V) from the previous photo. This photo shows the "licht und schatten' camouflage pattern on the side armor to good effect.

A whitewashed Sturmgeschutz IV from StuG.Abt.1012 which was knocked out in Losheimergraben, Belgium. Gasoline cans have been placed on the roadwheels, a sure sign that this vehicle is being prepared for destruction.

German Panzer IV/70(V) of an unknown unit sits abandoned guarding a snowy road somewhere in Belgium or Luxembourg in January 1945.

Two American soldiers from the 30th Infantry Division inspect a German Sturmgeschutz III on the road near St. Vith.

A German Sturmgeschutz III from H.St.Art.Brig.911 serving with Fuhrer Grenadier Brigade in Luxembourg during the Battle of the Bulge. A gun emplacement appears to be in the far left background. This vehicle has spare tracks on the fighting compartment and a shell hangs from the gun.

Near Marnach on the road to Dasburg and the Our River as the Germans retreated to their homeland, the armor columns became prime targets for Allied aircraft. This Panzer IV/70(V) lays in a crater after a direct hit from an aerial bomb. Unexploded ammunition from the vehicle lays on both sides of it in the massive crater.

Soldiers of the 702nd Tank Battalion or 80th Infantry Division inspect a Sturmgeschutz III belonging to Führer Grenadier Brigade, knocked out during the fighting south of Heiderscheid, Luxembourg on December 26, 1944.

Soldier of the 26th Infantry Division checks out a knocked out Sturmgeschutz III attached to the Fuhrer Grenadier Brigade near Eschdorf, Luxembourg on December 27, 1944. The 26th engaged the Germans in Eschdorf around December 23/24.

Two German Panzer IV/70(A)s from Fuhrer-Begleit Brigade lay snow covered next to a curious pig after being knocked out by elements of the 11th Armored Division around the town of Chenogne, Belgium in late December 1944.

Engineers of the 291st Combat Engineer Battalion defuse a booby trap they found in this German Sturmgeschutz III belonging to Panzer Brigade 150 near Geromont, Belgium on January 16, 1945. Stars were painted on the vehicle to try and make it look like an American armored vehicle.

Lt. H.G Foltin searches a German Sturmgeschutz IV of Panzerjager Abteilung 348 for booby traps. The location was noted as the road to Ambleve in late January 1945. Lt. Foltin was with the 2895th Engineer Technical Intelligence Team whose job was to inspect enemy vehicles and equipment for booby traps and also to learn more about the enemy's technological capabilities.

A Sturmgeschutz III, probably from the 2nd Panzer Division lays knocked out in a bomb crater in Noville, Belgium in January 1945. The side skirt armor on the side shows the camouflage paint pattern that had been applied to this vehicle. The 11th Armored Division claimed credit for this knocked out vehicle.

GIs of the 30th Infantry Division check out a snow covered and abandoned Sturmgeschutz III near St. Vith Belgium near the end of the Battle of the Bulge.

A German self-propelled gun sits knocked out on the road to St. Vith a victim of the advance of the 7th Armored Division in this sector around January 23, 1945.

An American tanker inspects what is left of a Panzerjager 38 (t) after it suffered a massive explosion.

A German Panzerjager 38 (t) sits still smoldering near the town of Wallerode just outside St.Vith. The 7th Armored Division was in action in this area and would have been responsible for destroying this vehicle.

GI of the 16th Infantry Regiment, 1st Infantry Division inspects a German Sturmgeschutz IV that has been over onto its side, either by the force of an explosion or by a bulldozer when moved off the road. The location is the outskirts of Ambleve, Belgium in late January 1945.

A German self-propelled gun sits in a barn in Wilwerwiltz, Luxembourg after being captured by the 80th Infantry Division. The caption stated that the vehicle was found in the barn and it was in there for repairs.

The frozen body of a German soldier lays in front of a snow covered German Jagdpanther outside of Bullingen, Belgium.

An M5a1 light tank belonging to Company D, 37th Tank Battalion of the 4th Armored Division heads towards Bastogne on December 27, 1944. This battalion was commanded by Colonel Creigton Abrams.

Two tankers of the 759th Light Tank Battalion eat and smoke over a fire near their M5A1 light tank while guarding a VII Corps outpost in Belgium, December 30, 1944. The 759th was a battalion comprised of M5A1 light tanks only.

Another photo of a 759th Tank Battalion crewmen trying to stay warm in the Belgium winter of 1944. Their M5A1 has some branches resting on it to break up the shape of the tank from enemy observers.

Belgian woman poses on top of a M5A1 light tank of the 86th Cavalry Reconnaissance Squadron of the 6th Armored Division as it stopped for a rest in Habay-la-Neuve, Belgium on December 29 while on its way towards the Bastogne sector.

The cameraman has moved closer to the M5A1light tank and some other local Belgian women have joined the tank for a quick drink and celebratory photo.

A dead German soldier lays propped up on a wheeled cart next to a M5A1 light tank of the 33rd Armored Regiment, 3rd Armored Division in Baneux, Belgium on January 5, 1945. The light tank has a lucky four leaf clover painted on its hull side.

M5A1 light tanks of the 32nd Armored Regiment, 3rd Armored Division move down the street of Sart, Belgium on January 9, 1945.

An M31 Armored Recovery Vehicle or T2 attempts to pull out a stuck M5A1 light tank of the 3rd Armored Division that ran into a ditch near Houffalize, Belgium on January 9, 1945.

As German artillery begins to fall, soldiers take cover amongst M5a1 light tanks of Company B, 33rd Armored Regiment, Task Force Lovelady of the 3rd Armored Division in Langlir, Belgium on January 13, 1945.

Also in Langlir, Belgium, a GI moves up alongside a M5A1 light tank towards the enemy lines.

The M24 light tank, the replacement for the M5A1 began to make its appearance with units near the end of the Battle of the Bulge. Here soldiers with the 740th Tank Battalion and 82nd Airborn check out the new tank model. This one has already been whitewashed. It was armed with a heavier 75mm gun.

M5A1 light tanks of CCA of the 7th Armored Division move into Weims, Belgium on January 20, 1945.

Knocked out M5A1 light tanks of the 7th Armored sit lined up in a field in Belgium.

A unit from the 509th Parachute Infantry moves past a M5A1 light tank of the 7th Armored Division on the advance to St.Vith on January 24, 1945.

One of the newly arrived M24 light tanks gets introduced to men of the 39th Regiment, 9th Infantry Division at the end of the Bulge battles. Note the sign hanging from the front of the M24 that reads "American Tank M-24".

Two M5A1 light tanks that have been painted white rest in Dieuze, France on January 19, 1945. After bitter fighting by the 10th Armored Division in Belgium during the Bulge, they were pulled out of the line around January 17 and sent to France for rest and refitting.

Outside Bastogne, tanks of the 37th Tank Battalion, 4th Armored Division deploy and spread out over the snowy fields. Closest to camera is an M5a1 light tank named "Dauntless".

Tankers of a M4 medium tank from the 66th Armored Regiment, 2nd Armored Division and a crew of an anti-tank unit of the 84th Infantry Division point to sky and watch friendly American bombers pass over on their way to knock out German supply lines on January 10, 1945.

M4 medium tank rolls through Belgian town on the way to the front during the early days of the Ardennes Offensive, December 21, 1944.

M4A1 medium tank of the 32nd Armored Regiment, Task Force Kane of the 3rd Armored Division stands guard at a roadblock on the Manhay road on December 23, 1944. Copious amounts of straw have been added to the tank for camouflage.

In Hotton, Belgium, the scene of bitter fighting in the early days of the Bulge, a 3rd Armored Division soldiers adds straw to his M4 medium tank for extra concealment from German soldiers.

Lt John Modrack of the 33rd Armored Regiment checks out a knocked out American M4 medium tank from Company G, 32nd Armored Regiment that had been destroyed in Hotton, Belgium during the fierce battles there.

75th Infantry Division soldiers march past a 2nd Armored Division medium tank in Bussionville, Belgium on December 26, 1944. The men are with the 291st Infantry Regiment.

Medium tank of the 19th Tank Battalion, 9th Armored Division rolls past an American jeep towards Bastogne in the early days of the Ardennes Offensive.

Section of M4A1 medium tanks of the 2nd Armored Division carry infantry towards Frandeux, Belgium on December 27, 1944 to battle the German 2nd Panzer Division.

3 photo sequence outside of Manhay, Belgium on December 27, 1944, tankers of the 7th Armored Division in either a M4(105) or M4A3 (105) assault gun watch American planes strafe German lines which aren't far away at all. The tank belongs to the 40th Tank Battalion of the 7th Armored Division. Tree branches and sprigs have been applied for camouflage to the tank that has been placed in a dug out position.

M4 (105mm) assault guns from the 750th Tank Battalion provide fire support for troops near Manhay, Belgium on December 30, 1944.

In the town of Trou-de-Bra on January 3, 1945 is a M4A3E2 (75) assault tank or "Jumbo" carrying soldiers from the 82nd Airborne Division to prepare to take the next town in the American counterattack that began in early January.

GI from the 4th Armored Division inspects two holes from German armor piercing shells that have knocked out this M4 medium tank in the Bastogne sector. The tank has duckbill track extenders and the extra armor welded on the tank failed to provide much extra protection. It appears the Germans used the American star as an aiming point.

The same tank from the previous photo as it is prepared to be moved back to an ordnance repair facility by a M25 tank transporter.

Crew members of an M4 (105) assault gun from HQ Company, 17th Tank Battalion, 7th Armored Division fine tune their vehicle while have just been taken off alert status. The tank has evergreen branches for extra camouflage and logs on the side for extra traction on the ground when needed.

M4 medium tank of the 740th Tank Battalion while supporting the 82nd Airborne Division moves down a snowy road towards the front lines near Herresbach, Belgium.

M4 medium tank of the 4th Armored moves up past an American machine gun position outside Bastogne on January 3, 1945. Many of the official captions at this time were very general with their location and would simply say "around Bastogne".

An American M4 medium tank with a fresh coat of whitewash sits outside a building with another tank inside of it. The unit is unknown but the location is Grand Halleux, Belgium in January 1945.

Knocked out M4A3 medium tank from the 6th Armored Division sits with one side of its tracks missing in Hompre, Belgium on the outskirts of Bastogne. The soldier is pointing to where a German armor piercing shell hit on the turret base.

M4 medium tanks of the 35th Tank Battalion, 4th Armored Division move past Bastogne near Sainlex on December 31, 1944 to widen the front around that sector once the city was reached and the encirclement broken.

M4 tanks of the 2nd Armored Division, the front one with duckbill extenders installed on the tracks for better traction support the 84th Infantry Division around Amonines, Belgium on January 2, 1945.

An American M4A1 (76) medium tank with sandbagged frontal protection moves up to meet the German forces near La Fosse sector of Belgium on January 3, 1945.

M4 (105) assault guns from a HQ company of the 2nd Armored Division provide fire support to attacking troops in Belgium.

Tank crews of a M4A1 (76) repair tracks in the woods near Amonines, Belgium during a break in the action. The men are from Company F, 66th Armored Regiment, 2nd Armored Division.

Taken just yards away from the previous photo is another tank from Company F, 66th Armored, 2nd Armored Division taking shelter in the snowy woods while according to the caption, the Germans were only 300 yards away.

M4 medium tank of 1st Battalion, 33rd Armored Regiment, 3rd Armored Division struggles to maneuver a small slope in the snow in Baneux, Belgium during an attack by the division in that area on January 5, 1945.

M4 medium tank attached to the 35th Infantry Division prepares to move over an area prepared with tree limbs and logs to prevent it from sliding down the hill in a small village on the outskirts of Bastogne on January 4, 1945.

A British IC Firefly has lost traction and slid down a hill in a village in Belgium in January 1945. The tank is supporting the British Division and the circle on the hull indicates it part of C Squadron of a British armored battalion.

A common scene in the icy Ardennes, a medium tank, this one part of the 2nd Armored Division has slid off the road into a small ditch on the side and waits for help to be pulled out.

Knocked out tanks of the 11th Armored Division prepare to be moved out by M25 tank transporters on January 4, 1945. These tank were knocked out near Bastogne during the American counterattack.

An American M4A3E2 (75) assault tank, "Jumbo" carrying soldiers of the 83rd Infantry Division moves up past Manhay, Belgium as the American counterattack in that area begins in early January 1945.

Soldier hands a 75mm shell to his fellow tanker of medium tank near Jodenville, Belgium on January 5, 1945. The tank is named "Charming Roma…" and is probably from the 11th Armored Division.

American tankers apply duckbill extenders on tracks for their M4A1 (76) medium tank from the 743rd Tank Battalion in December 1944.

M4 medium tanks of the 33rd Armored Regiment, 3rd Armored Division wait for another knocked out further down the road to be moved. The tanks are at pause on snowy tree lined road near Fraiture, Belgium on January 9, 1945.

M4 medium tank of probably the 2nd Armored Division stands guard next to a foxhole of infantrymen in the 75th Infantry Division sector around Beffe, Belgium on January 7, 1945.

M4 medium tank of the 2nd Armored Division covered in camouflage netting over its turret and hull is having trouble on the icy roads around Weris, Belgium about 7.5 km north of Erezee. The tank has a tow cable on the front to be helped out of the situation it has found itself.

M4A3E2 (75) assault tank of the 33rd Armored Regiment, 3rd Armored Division moves through Lierneux, Belgium past GIs of the 83rd Infantry Division. Different elements of the 83rd were attached to the 3rd Armored during the counter-offensive in January.

The caption for this photo mistakenly had this tank as a 3rd Armored Division tank in Lierneux, when it actually belongs to the 774th Tank Battalion which was attached to the 83rd Infantry during this time too. These tankers are taking a break in the action around January 9, 1945.

British M4A2 medium tanks of the Coldstream Guards, 5th Guards Armored Brigade, Guards Armored Division pull trucks up an icy road near Leignon, Belgium on January 8, 1945.

M4 medium tank named "Easy" of Company E, 66th Armored Regiment, 2nd Armored Division is getting tow cable attached from a M31 or T-2 armored recovery vehicle somewhere in the Ardennes on January 10, 1945.

During a rest in the action, Private Audry Ziegler of Company C, 17th Tank Battalion, 7th Armored Division applies white paint for camouflage to his medium tank on January 15, 1945. The paint was quick to put on and provided excellent camouflage in the whiteout environment.

M4 medium tank passes an ambulance as it heads to the front near Odeigne, Belgium on January 9, 1945.

Crew of a M4A1 medium tank of the 741st Tank Battalion, 2nd Infantry Division take a break outside their living quarters near Berg, Belgium. The crew has constructed a dugout right next to their tank. The 741st was in a rest period from January 1-11, 1945 after heavy fighting in Krinkelt-Rocherath.

Another tank of the 741st Tank Battalion in the Berg area on January 11. This M4 medium tank gets its 76mm gun cleaned before moving back to the front lines after a well deserved rest off the line.

In the 87th Infantry Division sector of the Ardennes, a M4A3 (75) medium tank of the 761st Tank Battalion has slipped off the road and turned on its side. A group of soldiers watch and determine the best way to turn the vehicle back over.

M4A3E8 (76) medium tank with muzzle brake of the 4th Armored Division covers a highway near Bastogne on January 8, 1945.

11th Armored Division vehicles prepare for action in supporting the 101st Airborne Division around the town of Foy on January 13, 1945. In addition to the M4 tanks in the foreground, in the back we can see halftracks, M7 105 GMC, a Piper Cub and even a Waco glider in the very far distance.

Crew of a M4A3 (76) medium tank of the 42nd Tank Battalion, 11th Armored Division cross their fingers for good luck after receiving their third tank in two weeks of fighting during the Bulge. From the official caption, the crew luckily didn't suffer any casualties.

An M4 medium tank of the 492nd Armored Field Artillery Battalion, 11th Armored Division being used by the forward observers moves towards Bastogne area on January 13, 1945.

An M4A3E2 (75) assault tank of the 743rd Tank Battalion and outfitted with whitewash paint, camouflage netting and duckbill extenders on the tracks moves through Malmedy, Belgium on January 13, 1945 on the way to the front lines. The 743rd Tank Battalion primarily supported the 30th Infantry Division.

M4 medium tank of the 15th Tank Battalion, 6th Armored Division moves up past Bastogne which according to the caption was only 7 miles to the west when this photo was taken on January 14, 1945. The tank has the typical whitewash camouflage of many American tanks during this time.

M4 medium tank of the 15th Tank Battalion, 6th Armored sits well camouflaged in the trees overlooking town of Benonchamps, Belgium while awaiting orders to move to the town which is 10 miles east of Bastogne.

M20 armored car of a reconnaissance unit moves past a knocked out M4 medium tank somewhere in the 90th Infantry Division sector of Luxembourg on January 14, 1945.

Minesweeper of the 17th Armored Engineer Battalion, 2nd Armored Division clears the road for 2nd Armored M4A1 medium tank on the move towards Houffalize, Belgium on January 16, 1945. The tank has sandbags on the glacis plate and grousers and duckbills on the tracks.

Freshly whitewashed M4 medium tank of the 32nd Armored Regiment, 3rd Armored Division in Belgium during January 1945.

Men of the 329th Infantry Regiment, 83rd Infantry Division set up a mortar in front of their medium tank of the 774th Tank Battalion outside of Langlir, Belgium on January 16, 1945.

M4 medium tank of the 6th Armored Division in Mageret, Belgium after being knocked out by a German bazooka.

M4 medium tank of the 745th Tank Battalion, attached to 1st Infantry Division has slipped off the road near Faymonville, Belgium on January 16, 1945. A dead German soldier lies frozen in the foreground.

GIs and tanks of the 3rd Army, probably of the 87th Infantry Division move up past St. Hubert in January 1945. The threat of snipers and enemy must not be too high as the soldiers standing on the tank look pretty at ease.

M4A3 (76) HVSS medium tank of Company B, 42nd Tank Battalion, 11th Armored Division moves out from Compiegne, Belgium on January 16. It is probably a replacement tank since it doesn't have whitewash yet.

Soldier from the 712th Tank Battalion, 90th Infantry Division brushes snow off his M4 medium tank outside of Doncols, Luxembourg on January 19, 1945. The tank is outfitted with duckbill connectors.

Another photo showing a medium tank of the 712th Tank Battalion getting snow brushed off after an overnight snowstorm in Doncols, Luxembourg.

Tankers of the 67th Armored Regiment, 2nd Armored Division work on their .50 caliber heavy machine gun in front of their heavily sandbagged M4 medium tank. This photo was taken January 12, 19345 near Les Tailles, Belgium during a break in the action.

Tank crew of Company A, 774th Tank Battalion, attached to 83rd Infantry Division apply whitewash paint to their medium tank in Joubieval, Belgium on January 17, 1945.

Crew of a M4A1 (76) medium tank from the 4th Armored Division apply tree branches and foliage to their whitewashed tank for better camouflage near Kiewelbach, Luxembourg on January 18, 1945.

Fuel truck that was refueling this M4 medium tank of the 7th Armored Division near St. Vitth became stuck in the heavy snow. Soldiers are digging snow out from around the tires.

Tanks of the 7th Armored Division move into bivouac position for the night after advancing all day. They are outside the town of Weims, Belgium on January 20, 1945.

M4(75) medium tank of the 68th Tank Battalion, 6th Armored Division that has lost its tracks lies knocked out along a house in Longvilly, Belgium on January 22, 1945. A M25 recovery vehicle is preparing to pull it away to either a repair facility or salvage location.

M4A3E2(75) assault tank of the 737th Tank Battalion moves up to the front past an American jeep, The Jumbo tank has been whitewashed and also has the sommerfield wire applied for easy installation of twigs and brush for camouflage.

An M4A3(76) medium tank of the 7th Armored Division lies knocked out and snow covered in Krombach, Belgium after making a stand at the crossroads there. The 7th Armored lost several tanks in its defense of Krombach when the Germans overran it on December 24.

M4 medium bulldozer tank pushes snow off a road somewhere in Belgium in January 1945. The heavy snow and whitewash paint on the M4 makes it nearly invisible. A column on infantry can be seen in the background.

An M4A3E2(75) assault tank has slipped off an embankment and ended stuck at the bottom, luckily it didn't turn over. The Jumbo like one of the 737th Tank Battalion pictured also has sommerfield matting installed.

Two M4A3(75) medium tanks of the 42nd Tank Battalion, 11th Armored Division warm themselves over a fire near Steinbach, Belgium on January 23, 1945. Given the date of the photo and the fact that these tanks are not whitewashed, they are probably replacement tanks after the losses the 11th suffered in the January battles.

Also, in Steinbach, a tanker from the 11th Armored Division makes sewing repairs to his clothing in front of his medium tank.

M4 medium tank of the 745th Tank Battalion, attached to the 1st Infantry Division stands guard at a roadblock in a Belgian village in January 1945.

Lt. Odens with the 7th Armored Division served as a field artillery forward observer assigned to an M4 medium tank. He is talking with other tanks and artillery of the division around St.Vith on January 25.

M4 medium tanks of the 40th Tank Battalion, 7th Armored Division sit outside St.Vith on January 24 1945 as operations in that area were coming to a close. Between the snow covered trees and their whitewash paint, the tanks would be hard to spot from a distance.

The Germans were happy to turn captured American tanks to their use, especially with their armor shortages. Here is an American M4A3 medium tank that had been captured by the Germans and then knocked out by Allied aircraft near Dasburg, where the German 7th Army was retreating back to Germany.

Another M4A3 medium tank captured by the Germans and put to use. This tank was knocked out by the 10th Armored Division in January. The Germans tried to paint over the white American star and added a small German cross to the front. The location is somewhere in Luxembourg.

Not far from the previous photo, the cameraman found these two stuck and abandoned American medium tanks of the 10th Armored Division. They appear to be stuck past their tracks to the bottom of the hull and in some kind of ravine or creek bed that has thawed.

M4 medium tank of the 6th Armored Division lays knocked out around Longvilly, Belgium. A large internal explosion has caused the right side armor to literally peel away.

A closer view of the same tank. This photograph shows how the right side just peeled off and thus exposed the interior of the tank.

Crew of a M4(105) assault gun of the Headquarters Company of the 15th Tank Battalion, 6th Armored Division warm themselves around a fire outside Cherf, Belgium in January of 1945. Spent casings stand behind the men, blocking the wind from ruining their fire.

Another knocked out tank of the 6th Armored Division with one track missing and the other has been knocked off the running gear. Anti-tank hits appear to be on the front near where the assistant driver would have been sitting.

M4 tank of the 6th Armored Division, with an armor piercing shot that hit right in the turret, sits knocked out in a Belgian field. The exact unit of the division is not known but based on some other similar photos of knocked out tanks in this area it might be from the 69th Tank Battalion.

A cameraman as evidenced by his signal photographer patch on his arm points to the point of penetration on this turret of a M4 medium tank of the 6th Armored Division. Chains have been put on the turret to lift it off to see what may be salvageable in the tank.

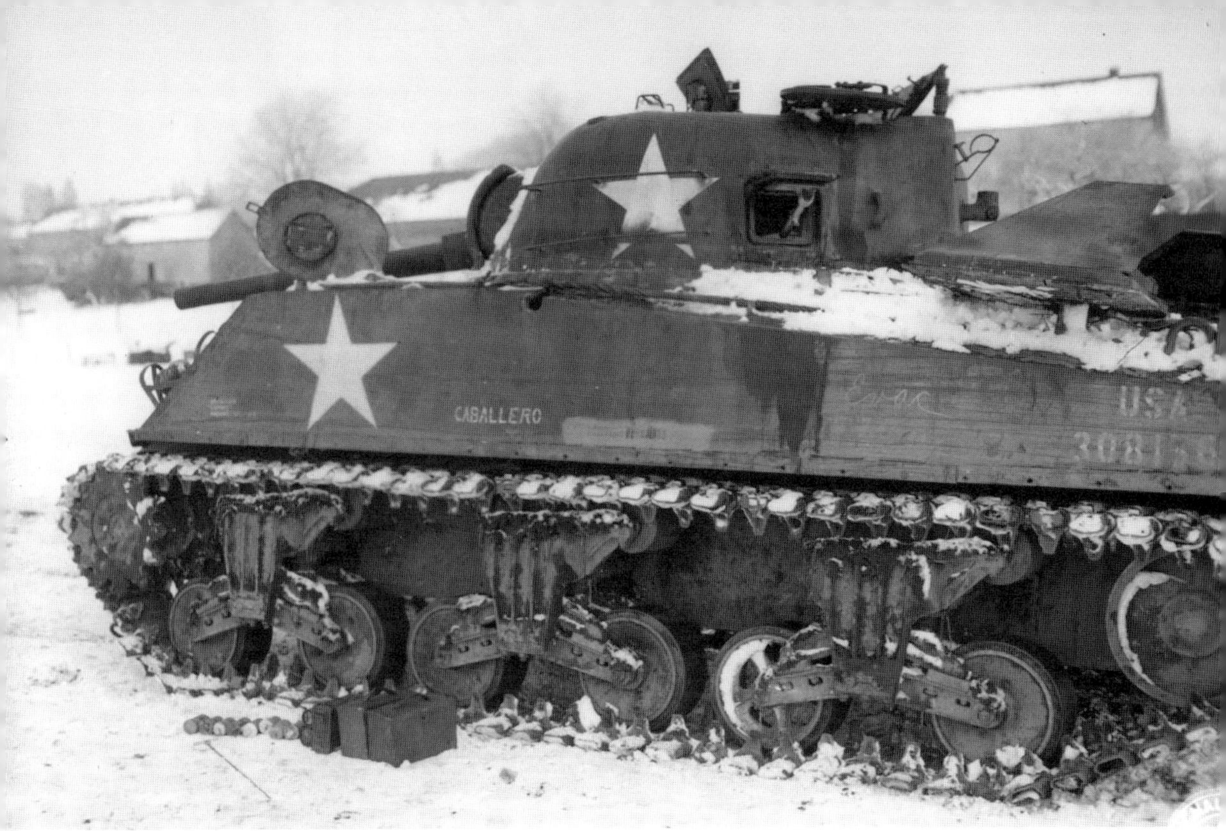

M4A3(75) medium tank named "Caballero" of the 69th Tank Battalion, 6th Armored Division shown under repairs after being damaged during the breakout from the Bastogne area in January 1945.

Two M4 medium tanks of the 15th Tank Battalion, 6th Armored Division sit destroyed near Longvilly where they were knocked out around January 15 during the operations to move out of the Bastogne area.

Tank 50 of the 15th Tank Battalion, 6th Armored Division would have been in Company B. This medium tank is the one on the right from the previous photo.

The photographer with the 6th Armored Division might have been on an assignment to take photos of the knocked out tanks of the division for after-action reports and analysis because he took several. Here a tank named "Bucko" sits knocked out after receiving an anti-tank round to its hull side.

A Mine Exploder T1E1 Roller (earthworm) with the 17th Armored Engineer Battalion, 2nd Armored Division clears the way for a column of 2nd Armored tanks as they move towards Houffalize in January 1945.

A great side view of another T1E1, this one working with the 1st Infantry Division as it moves to another area to search for and disarm German mines.

T1E3/M1 Roller (Aunt Jemima) mine exploder with the 738th Tank Battalion moves past a German cemetery near Recht, Belgium in January 1945.

Another 738th Tank Battalion special vehicle, this one the T1E1 mine exploder model sits near a barn outside Ligneuville, Belgium in January 1945. A soldier is moving communications wire so that the tank doesn't move them when it leaves its position.

GIs inspect a German PzKpfw IV that has had its turret blown off. The tank belonged to Kampfgruppe Peiper and was probably destroyed by M10s of the 644th Tank Destroyer Battalion on December 17 near Wirtzfeld.

In the town of Dom Butgenbach lies a German PzKpfw IV of the 12th SS Panzer Division that was destroyed by a M36 90mm GMC of the 634th Tank Destroyer Battalion. Maybe the M36 to the left of the German tank was the one who did the deed.

A German PzKpfw IV of the 1116th Panzer Division burns in the town of Hotton after the Germans were stopped there by various elements of the 3rd Armored Division. According to the caption, this tank was burned to prevent its use by the Germans if recaptured but this footage was also used in a signal corps movie reel so perhaps it was burned for dramatic effect.

Once the ammunition inside a tank catches fire, massive explosions can cause the turret to be lifted off the hull. This German PzKpfw IV was attached to Kampfgruppe Mauck of the 15th Panzergrenadier Division and was knocked out by the 101st Airborne outside Bastogne in December 1944.

PzKpfw IV appears to have had a explosion in its rear engine compartment and it is hard to make sense of the turret, and schurzen. No details on unit or location other than "Ardennes 1945".

A German PzKpfw IV of the 7th Company of the 1st SS Panzer Regiment, 1st SS Panzer Division sits snow covered while inspected by GIs of the 35th Infantry Division outside Lutrebois, Belgium. This tank was knocked out on December 30 in the attempts to take Bastogne.

American M36 90mm GMC of the 703rd Tank Destroyer Battalion moves past a knocked out German PzKpfw of either the 2nd or 9th SS Panzer Divisions around Langlir, Belgium in January 1945. Notice the difference between a whitewashed tank and the M36 that hasn't been whitewashed.

A whitewashed M3A1 half-track of the 21st Armored Infantry Battalion, 11th Armored Division, passes a destroyed German PzKpfw IV in the village of Foy, Belgium, in early January.

A German PzKpfw IV possibly of the 15th Panzergrenadier Division sits on a road with its contents from boxes inside and outside of it strewn about. The location is Luxembourg in January 1945.

A staged photograph for sure. GIs of the 90th Infantry Division move up against a German Panzerbefehlswagen IV "command tank" of the 12th SS Panzer Division in Luxembourg in January 1945.

Two photos of the same German PzKpfw IV tank of the 33rd Panzer Regiment knocked out in Foy, Belgium. Note the side skirts of wire mesh intended to stop bazooka rounds.

GIs carefully inspect a German PzKpfw IV resting gingerly on a hillside outside Goesdorf, Luxembourg on January 9. The parent unit of the tank was the Fuhrer Grenadier Brigade.

In Houffalize after the Germans had retreated, the Americans found this German Pz.Beob.Wg III command vehicle. An older tank for this part of the war, it probably belonged to the 9th Panzer Division that was engaged in this area.

The two photos are from the same German PzKpfw V "Panther" tank of the 116th Panzer Division. This tank was numbered 322 and was lost in the garden of a house in Hotton on December 21 to the 3rd Armored Division. Here, tankers of the 3rd Armored examine the iron beast after knocking it out.

Cameraman Bill Cummings of the 166th Signal Photographic Company stands next to a German Panther knocked out probably in Luxembourg and possibly from the Fuhrer Grenadier Brigade.

A staged photograph as a member of signal corps photographic team walks a German past a burning Panther of the 12th SS Panzer Division near the twin villages of Krinkelt-Rocherath on December 17, 1944.

The same Panther tank as in the previous photo, tactical number 126. The tank was knocked out by medium tanks of the 741st Tank Battalion who were supporting the 2nd and 99th Infantry Divisions in this area.

Tanks of the 12th SS littered the area around the twin villages of Krinkelt-Rocherath which was the scene of vicious fighting at the beginning of the Ardennes Offensive. Here two more Panthers sit burning with the one in the foreground, number 318 having had its gun barrel blown off.

American tankers of the 3rd Armored Division inspect a German PzKpfw V of the 116th Panzer Division in Hotton with a PzKpfw IV behind next to a damaged house. The battles in Hotton were some of the more fierce in the opening days for the 3rd Armored Division in the Bulge.

Soldiers of the 702nd Tank Battalion and 80th Infantry Division look over a knocked out PzKpfw V around Heiderscheid, Luxembourg. The Panther was from the Fuhrer Grenadier Brigade and has spare tracks around its turret.

A US truck moves past a German PzKpfw V of the 2nd Panzer Division that had been knocked out by the 2nd Armored Division in the area around Ciney, Belgium in December of 1944.

More victims of the American 3rd Armored Division. Three PzKpfw Vs of the 9th Panzer Division that tried to defend the town of Humain against the Americans, sit knocked out in a field outside the town on December 27, 1944.

Two photos of the same tank that show great detail from the front and side. The tank is number 221, a PzKpfw V belonging to the 1st SS Panzer Division, Kampfgruppe Peiper to be exact in La Gleize, Belgium after the Germans retreated from the town and left several tanks and other armored vehicles.

Two photos of the same German PzKpfw V, taken a few weeks apart. The tank is from the 2nd SS Panzer Division and was knocked out at the crossroads in Manhay in December 1944. A few weeks later, Signal Corps cameraman Harold Roberts, covering the 3rd Armored Division had his photo taken in front of the Panther which was now covered in snow.

The 2nd SS Panzer Division rushed into Manhay and Grandmenil on December 24th and pushed back elements of the 3rd Armored Division. A few days later though, the 3rd Armored sent Task Force McGeorge to the area and the towns were retaken by armor and infantry. Here a GI of the 75th Infantry inspects one of the Das Reich Panthers in that area.

American M4 medium tank rolls past a knocked out PzKpfw V of the 2nd SS Panzer Division near Grandmenil, Belgium.

Series of three photos taken by the 238th Combat Engineer Company of a few of the five Panther tanks they knocked out by an extensive minefield the unit planted outside Grandmenil, Belgium on December 25. The tanks are from the 2nd SS Panzer Division. The last photo shows that the crew might have attempted to repair the tank as a jack is in position on the rear tow pintle.

GI from the 6th Armored Division looks at the damage to a PzKpfw V of the Panzer Regiment of Panzer Lehr Division. The tank was knocked out with another from its unit on the road heading into Neffe, Belgium.

This photograph shows the other Panther from Panzer Regiment 130 that was lost on the road to Neffe. This tank was knocked out by a mine. The tank from the previous photo can be seen in the rear of this photo.

GIs on a 3rd Armored Division tank prepare to pass a snow covered Panther of the 2nd SS Panzer Division in Manhay after the Germans had lost several tanks there.

Another German PzKpfw lost in Manhay, Belgium. Here, American soldiers check out this particular tank that has either fallen off the side of the road or been pushed off by an American bulldozer.

Two American soldiers sit on a knocked out German PzKpfw V of the 2nd SS Panzer Division in Grandmenil after the fierce battles of late December 1944 there.

Two photos of another German PzKpfw V of the 2nd SS Panzer Division knocked out and lost in Manhay. These photos show how much snow has fallen since they were knocked out and an American bulldozer belonging to a engineer units moves the tank off the road to make room for traffic.

American jeep moves past a German Panther "somewhere near Houffalize" according to the official caption. Sometimes the captions made by the official cameramen were very detailed, and sometimes quite vague.

M5a1 light tank moves past an abandoned German PzKpfw V of the 2nd SS Panzer Division on a snowy and hilly road.

Series of three photos of the same tank, the first two taken a day before the last. Soldiers with the 83rd Infantry Division check out a knocked out German PzKpfw V of the 9th SS Panzer Division in Langlir, Belgium on January 13, 1945. The tank is numbered 121 and was knocked out by a 57mm anti-tank crew of the 331st Infantry, 83rd Infantry Division who were working with the 3rd Armored Division at this time. Note the penetrating hole right under the numbers on the turret, well placed shot by the gun crew.

121

Two photos of the same German PzKpfw V of the 9th SS Panzer Division in the woods near Bovigny, Belgium around January 17, 1945. The first photo shows men of the 83rd Infantry Division running communications wire through the trees. The second photo shows an M4 medium tank of the 774th Tank Battalion moving past the same Panther.

Another tank of the 9th SS Panzer Division. A PzKpfw V sits alongside a destroyed building near Houffalize. The Panther tank has been destroyed by an internal explosion.

American tankers from the 3rd Armored Division, probably from Task Force Kane, check out the rear of another PzKpfw V of the 9th SS Panzer Division. This tank was knocked out in the fierce fighting in the town of Sterpigny, Belgium.

American ambulance moves past a destroyed German PzKpfw V that was probably pushed off the road on its side by an American bulldozer. This photograph was taken in the 90th Infantry Division sector on January 22, 1945.

Another 9th SS Panzer Division PzKpfw V that was destroyed in the Battle of the Bulge. This vehicle was photographed near Sart-lez-St.Vith on January 23. The 40th Tank Battalion of the 7th Armored reported knocking out German tanks in this area in December and this could be one of its victims.

Destroyed German PzKpfw V numbered 125 of the 12th SS Panzer Regiment sits knocked out at the main crossroads in Krinkelt-Rocherath. The tank was knocked out on December 18 by the 644th Tank Destroyer Battalion.

Just 200 meters north-east of where the previous photo was taken, sit two more German Panthers of the 12th SS Panzer Division. These same tanks were photographed at the beginning of the battle and shown previously in this chapter.

As noted previously, the twin villages of Krinkelt-Rocherath were littered with 12th SS Panzer Division tank wrecks. Here sit two more knocked PzKpfw Vs, both with foliage applied for camouflage.

German PzKpfw V, numbered 301 from the 2nd Panzer Division sits abandoned, probably due to mechanical issues near Clervaux, Luxembourg. The photo was taken around January 26, 1945 when the 26th Infantry Division retook the town at the end of the Ardennes Campaign.

A German PzKpfw V modified to look like an American M-10 tank destroyer under the units commanded by Otto Skorzeny in the Ardennes battles to try and confuse the Americans. This particular one was disabled by a mine and is being towed away near Malmedy almost a month after it was knocked out.

German Panzer PzKpfw V of the 9th Panzer Division being inspected by American soldiers after being knocked out in Humain, Belgium on December 28. The soldiers are from the 83rd Infantry Division

Two Panther tanks, probably from the 9th Panzer Division sit knocked out in the woods around Marnach, Luxembourg on the way to Dasburg and the German border. Allied aircraft had a plethora of targets in this area as the Germans frantically made their way back to the German border.

German Panther from the Fuhrer Grenadier Brigade was knocked out in the village of Eschdorf, Luxembourg in December when up against the 26th Infantry Division and supporting elements. In the foreground, a member of the photographic team takes movie footage with his camera.

An ETO technical report was made when a German Bergepanther armored recovery vehicle was captured in the town of Morhet which is southwest of Bastogne, The vehicle belonged to the Panzer Lehr Division and was sent back to the States for further evaluation.

A German PzKpfw VI or Tiger I from Schwere Panzer Abteilung (s.Pz.Abt) 506 sits knocked out somewhere in Luxembourg near the command post of the 357th Infantry Regiment of the 90th Infantry Division as evidenced by the sign to the right of the tank.

Also in the 90th Infantry Division sector near Oberwampach, Lunxembourg on January 21, 1945, two mortar observers with the 90th Infantry Division in front of a snow covered Tiger 1 of s.Pz.Abt 506.

A German King Tiger column from SS-s.Pz.Abt 501 passes a line of American prisoners with the town of Merlscheid in the background. The 501st was attached to Kampfgruppe Peiper for the Battle of the Bulge. This photo came from captured German stills thus the marks on some of the soldiers faces by the American sensor.

King Tiger numbered 105 from the SS-s.Pz.Abt 501 that became stuck in rubble on the narrow streets of Stavelot on December 18. Many German tanks at this part of the war were lost because of lack of fuel or mechanical issues rather than being knocked out in action.

A front view of Tiger 105 in Stavelot showing how it became stuck on a pile of rubble from the destroyed house in Stavelot.

King Tiger 332 from SS-s.Pz.Abt 501 was photographed near Coo, Belgium in December where it was abandoned due to technical problems. The tank was already abandoned when Task Force Lovelady from the 3rd Armored Division stumbled upon it. This tank was then shipped to Spa for several photos before being shipped of the States. It now sits at the US Armor Museum at Fort Benning, GA.

Tiger numbered 104 of the SS-s.Pz.Abt 501, Kampfgruppe Peiper sits snow covered in a narrow lane in La Gleize, Belgium on December 28, 1944 after being left there by the Germans. Men of the 298th Combat Engineer Battalion are inspecting it. Note the machine gun bullets draped over the barrel for dramatic effect. Weeks later this tank would be used for target practice with bazookas and panzerfausts by men of the 82nd Airborne Division.

The following three photos show the same Tiger II, numbered 204 of SS-S.Pz.Abt 501 that ran out of fuel and was left on the side of the road near Gue on Christmas Eve after Kampfgruppe Peiper had left La Gleize. It was then taken over by American troops who attempted to drive it to a collection point but then it broke down on a side of a road near Ruy. Here an American soldier stands on the side for a closer look, the number 204 is clearly visible.

Soldiers of an ordnance unit warm themselves over a roadside fire while trying to figure out how to move the broken down Tiger II back to a vehicle collection point.

The immense size of the Tiger II, including its 88mm gun is evident in this photo as it takes up most of the road and dwarfs the American ambulance of the 30th Infantry Division that is passing it.

King Tiger 312 of SS-s.Pz.Abt 501 was lost near Goronne on January 7, 1945. Here GIs of the 82nd Airborne string signal wire over the knocked out tank while some curious Belgian ladies stroll by.

Series of three photos taken by and showing an official signal corps cameraman taking measurements of a Tiger II of s.Pz.Abt 506. The location is Moinet, Belgium in the 6th Armored Division sector. In this photo the men are measuring the length of the vehicle.

The signal corps photographer is identifiable by his official patch on his jacket sleeve. He is measuring the width of the Tiger II tracks.

In this photo, the cameraman is leaning over the front of the turretless Tiger II to examine the zimmerit application and the multiple anti-tank hits it has suffered, but none appear to have penetrated the thick armor.